WOODWORK
FOR THE GARDEN
Including 16 easy-to-build projects

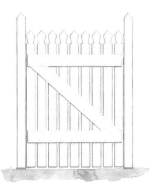

ALAN & GILL BRIDGEWATER

NEW
HOLLAND

This paperback edition first published in 2008 by
New Holland Publishers (UK) Ltd

London • Cape Town • Sydney • Auckland

Garfield House, 86–88 Edgware Road, London W2 2EA, United Kingdom
www.newhollandpublishers.com

80 McKenzie Street, Cape Town, 8001, South Africa

Unit 1, 66 Gibbes Street, Chatswood, NSW 2067, Australia

218 Lake Road, Northcote, Auckland, New Zealand

10 9 8 7 6 5 4 3 2 1

ISBN 978 1 84773 166 1

Editorial Direction: Rosemary Wilkinson
Project Editor: Clare Johnson
Production: Hazel Kirkman

Designed and created for New Holland by AG&G BOOKS
Designer: Glyn Bridgewater
Illustrator: Gill Bridgewater
Project design: Alan and Gill Bridgewater
Photography: AG&G Books and Ian Parsons
Editor: Fiona Corbridge
Woodwork: Alan and Gill Bridgewater, William Del Tufo and Richard Cope

AG&G Books would like to thank Anglian Timber Ltd for their help.

Reproduction by Pica Digital Pte Ltd, Singapore
Printed and bound in Malaysia by Times Offset (M) Sdn. Bhd.

Contents

Part 1: Techniques 8

Part 2: Projects 32

Introduction

One fine summer's day, Gill and I were busy in the workshop enjoying our woodwork, but at the same time desperately wishing that we could be outside in the garden soaking up the sun. Then we realized that we could have the best of both worlds: we could in fact be outside building really adventurous woodworking projects for the garden. We downed tools and wandered around the garden considering the possibilities. I immediately thought about constructing a picnic table I had been dreaming about, and Gill had a Victorian tool shed in her sights. Better still, garden woodwork would be able to make use of relatively low-cost, rough-sawn wood straight from the sawmill, and we would only require basic tools.

The ambition of this book is to share with you all the delights of working with wood to build beautiful creations for the garden. Each project follows the steps of collecting together tools and materials, considering the design, and building. We describe how the component parts are cut and fitted, colourwash illustrations show how the structures are built, and photographs demonstrate how best to achieve the step-by-step procedures; in fact, we take you through all the stages of designing, making and finishing.

So, if you like the idea of spending time out in the garden doing woodwork, which will add to the interest and functionality of your garden, you will get a lot of enjoyment from this book. You may have ambitions to sit on your very own bench to have a coffee, to eat lunch on a picnic table, or to nestle under a romantic arch. You may long for an arbour where you can canoodle with your partner, or perhaps your children have always nagged you for a playhouse. Try one or two projects during the summer, then dream about all the garden woodwork that you are going to build next year!

Best of luck.

Alan & Gill

HEALTH AND SAFETY

Many woodworking procedures are potentially dangerous, so before starting work on the projects, check through the following list:

• Make sure that you are fit and strong enough for the task ahead. If you have doubts, ask your doctor for specific advice.
• When you are building sheds, arbours, pergolas and other large structures, you will need to ask others to help you assemble the components towards the end of the project.

• When operating power tools, read the safety instructions supplied with the tool and wear the appropriate protective gear. A dust-mask and pair of goggles are usually adequate, and if the machine is noisy, wear ear defenders.
• Never operate electric tools, such as a drill or saw, if you are overtired.
• Use power saws extremely carefully. Keep your fingers well away from the blade and use a stick of scrap wood for holding or pushing through short lengths of wood.

Part 1: Techniques

Designing and planning

Whatever the size of your garden or its situation, a well thought-out woodwork project will undoubtedly make it a more exciting and dynamic place. You don't have to have loads of experience as a woodworker in order to follow our projects successfully: if you have the correct tools, choose your wood with care, and spend time carefully designing and planning the whole exercise, you will be sure to get good results.

FIRST CONSIDERATIONS

- Do you have a local sawmill, where you can buy rough-sawn, pre-treated wood suitable for building sheds, fences and gates?
- Will the sawmill deliver small quantities of wood, or are you going to fetch it yourself? Do you have a trailer or a suitable rack on the roof of your car?
- Do children and pets use your garden, and if so, is their presence going to affect your choice of project?
- Where are you going to do the woodwork? Are you going to work close to the house, perhaps on a patio or in a yard, or are you going to work on the lawn?
- If you are building a structure such as a shed or arbour, are you going to set it up on levelled blocks or bricks, or are you going to lay a concrete slab?
- Are your neighbours going to be concerned about the siting of a project? If this is a possibility, it's a good idea to involve them at the planning stage.
- Are you going to need help with lifting? If you plan to build the Victorian Tool Shed (see page 108), will you do the construction close to the site, or will you get help to move the panels once they have been built?

Choosing a suitable project

When you have decided what you'd like to build, the next step is to consider the project in terms of the site you have in mind. Is your chosen project perhaps too large for the site? Will you have to move a drain? Will the project upset the way that you and the family currently use the garden?

Are there any narrow gateways that might restrict access when installing a project that you have built away from its eventual site? Are there any shrubs that need to be cut back to allow the project to be put in position? Would it be a good idea to mend and paint your fences before you build a shed? Are there any local restrictions related to the building of sheds?

So, our advice is to choose your projects with great care, and to involve your family (and neighbours if the projects could conceivably affect them, for example the height of your planned structure may obstruct their views) in decision-making, before going ahead and enjoying the building experience.

Planning the project

Whatever your choice of project, whether it is the Rabbit Ark (see page 94) or the Classic Pergola (see page 100), it is vital to plan it out to the last detail, otherwise you can be caught out by unforseen difficulties. If you are thinking about building a large, fixed project such as the Victorian Tool Shed (see page 108), draw a plan of your garden complete with the house, paths, flowerbeds, trees and hedges. Mark in the trajectory of the sun as it arcs across the garden. Will the new shed cast shadows that will affect the flowerbeds? Will it necessitate the building of a new path so the shed can be reached easily from the house?

Keep asking yourself questions. If you have any doubts about how the shed will look when it has been erected, it's a good idea to peg out the site and build a large batten, board and string framework to the size of the shed. When the mock-up is in position, walk around it and consider how it relates to the rest of the garden. Live with it for a few days and see if it affects your family's movement around the garden.

Before you dig deep holes or bang in spiked metal post supports (for a fence, gate or pergola), it is important to avoid potential problems by studying site plans, testing the ground or making trial holes. If you suspect that there might be an underground structure such as a water main, drain or power supply, start by gently and carefully probing the ground with a metal rod. If it slides into the ground easily, the site is clear, but if it meets an obstruction, you must consider digging a trial hole to see what the problem is, or opt to move the project anyway.

Buying the right tools and materials

The best strategy, when building up a tool collection, is to get yourself a basic kit, and then buy specialist tools if the need arises.

When sourcing your materials, on no account consider using pre-packed, planed wood from the local DIY store. Not only would it treble your costs, but its overly smooth finish makes it unsuitable for the projects in this book. You must order rough-sawn wood from a local sawmill. Shop around for the best price and then order in bulk. When you go to the sawmill, ask to see their waste pile, just in case there is a bargain to be had. For example, with the feather-edged boarding, we were able to cut costs dramatically by using wood from a heap of random lengths. When selecting your wood, make sure that the finish is suitable. For instance, you must not use pressure-treated wood for the playhouse, because of the toxic nature of some preservatives.

WOODWORK DESIGNS FOR THE GARDEN

Rabbit ark
The perfect place to keep your rabbits and great fun for children

Picket gate
A decorative gate that leads the way to another area of the garden

Potting table
Tucked away in a corner so that you can pot your plants in peace

Victorian tool shed
A useful shed – just right for the mower

Multi-shaped decking
A movable patio area that will fit in many areas of the garden

Picket fence
The ideal feature to complement the romantic arch

Classic arbour
The perfect place for a tête-à-tête

Wheeled bench
For two people, with a table in-between. Easy to move about the garden

Corner patio planter
Located in a corner, as a design feature

Tiered patio planter
Placed against a wall, this is a clever design for displaying a lot of plants where space is tight

Treehouse
Children can play up here happily for hours, but an adult should never be too far away

Children's playhouse
A quiet and safe place for children to play

Romantic arch
A pretty feature that draws the eye

Decorative picnic bench
Located within easy reach of the house

Folding screen
An attractive feature that can be used to create distinct areas within a garden

Classic pergola
A bold, traditional design for displaying climbing plants

LEFT **This garden plan demonstrates how the projects in this book might be used to fill your garden with attractive woodwork designs.**

Tools

Always buy tools of the highest quality that you can afford. However, successful garden woodwork relies on controlling the wood while it is worked. To do this, you need a large space such as the lawn, two portable workbenches, and a sheet of plywood for setting out the component parts.

TOOLS FOR MEASURING AND MARKING

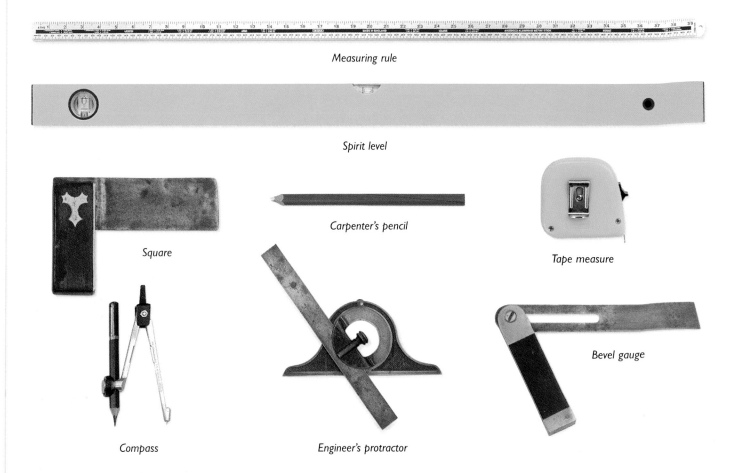

Measuring rule

Spirit level

Square

Carpenter's pencil

Tape measure

Compass

Engineer's protractor

Bevel gauge

Measuring

You need two measuring tools: a wood or metal measuring rule for sizing and marking joints, and a flexible tape measure for setting out the site plan for large projects (such as the Victorian Tool Shed on page 108) and for measuring long lengths of wood. We use an 8-metre tape for all the projects. If you can afford to spend a little extra, it's a good idea to use a fibreglass tape for trailing about the garden, because it is more resilient to the wear and tear of working on wet grass and with damp wood. Always wipe your measuring tool after use and put it away clean and dry.

Marking out

The tools for this are: a square for marking out right angles, a bevel gauge for setting out approximate angles, an engineer's protractor for setting out precise angles, a compass for drawing circles, and a clutch of good-quality carpenter's pencils for drawing on the wood. The flat lead in a carpenter's pencil not only keeps its point longer, but the rectangular section of the lead resists breaking – a really good idea when working on rough-sawn wood. Before you put your tools away, wipe them over with thin oil in order to protect them against damp and corrosion. We use olive oil, but alternatively you could use very thin engine or bicycle oil. On no account use old engine oil.

Levelling

For a project such as a shed, where the ground must be level, you require three tools: a flexible tape for setting out the site, a spade for digging away the earth, and a spirit level for checking vertical and horizontal levels. If you are going to get involved in building a concrete slab, you will also need a shovel and a garden rake.

TOOLS FOR CUTTING WOOD

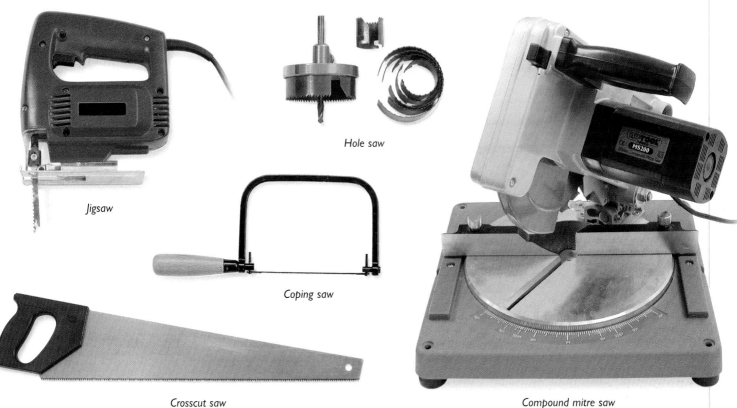

Jigsaw

Hole saw

Coping saw

Crosscut saw

Compound mitre saw

Sawing to size

Assuming that you purchase all your wood ready-sawn to a section size (sawn to the desired width and thickness), all you really need for the projects is a top-quality, hard-toothed, crosscut saw. Buy one that is described as "trade quality", and do not attempt to save money by opting for a bargain or secondhand saw. We purchased ours directly from the sawmill. Sawmill wood is generally green, wet, sappy and sometimes dirty, so it is best to get two crosscut saws – use one for cutting wood to length, and keep the other for cutting joints. To help ensure that the saw blades last, remove sticky sap with white spirit at the end of a day's work, and wipe the blade with olive oil or thin machine oil.

Sawing angles

While you can certainly make all straight and angled cuts with the crosscut saw already described, you can make life much easier – especially when cutting repeat angles – by obtaining an electric compound mitre saw. Not long ago, such saws were quite expensive, but now they are within reach of most people.

To use a compound mitre saw, set it on a level surface, either on a workboard or clamped in the jaws of a portable workbench. Adjust the blade to the desired angle, position the workpiece against the backstop, and then switch on the power and lower the blade to make the cut. Compound mitre saws are great tools for

> ### CAUTION
>
> The electric compound mitre saw is potentially an extremely dangerous tool. Never leave it unattended. If you have children, pull out the plug and lock the blade into the "down" position when not in use.

tasks such as cutting the tops of the pickets in the Picket Fence project (see page 42). When using a power tool such as this, always read the manufacturer's literature, follow all the safety rules, and work with a helper close at hand.

Sawing curves

The projects use three tools for cutting curves: a hand coping saw for small, tight curves in thin wood; an electric jigsaw for broad curves in thick wood; and an electric drill with a saw-toothed cutter (hole saw) for cutting large-diameter holes. We particularly enjoy using the jigsaw – it is an uncomplicated, very efficient, low-cost tool. To use it, you set the blade close to the start of the cut, with the bed of the tool resting flat on the wood, switch on the power, and then slowly advance the tool so that the cut runs slightly to the waste side of the drawn line. Remember not to snatch the tool from the workpiece while the blade is still moving. When you have made the cut, switch off the power, wait until the blade has come to a standstill, then lift the tool away. Always wear a dust-mask and a pair of safety goggles.

We used an electric drill with a saw-toothed cutter for cutting large-diameter holes in thick wood, but it wasn't an experience that we enjoyed. This tool combination does get the job done, but it is extremely noisy and juddery, and generates a lot of dust. If you feel nervous about using any of the power tools, it's a good idea to ask friends to help you.

TOOLS FOR MAKING JOINTS

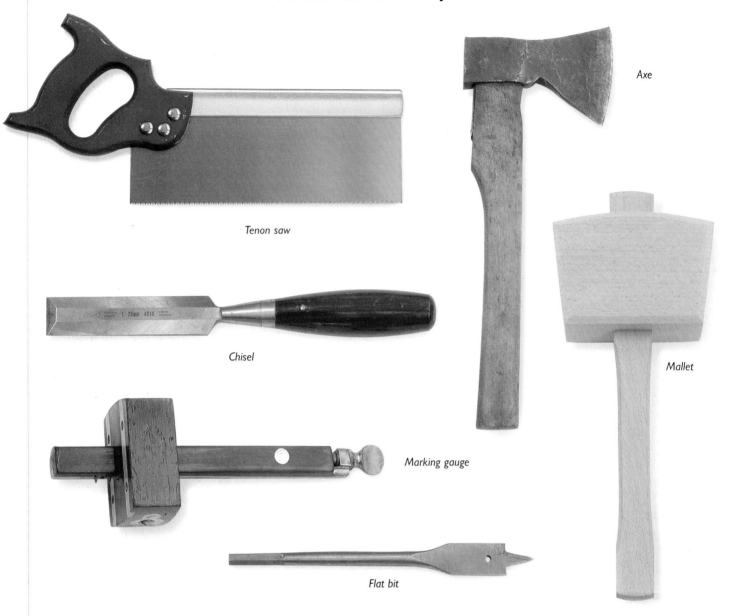

Tenon saw

Chisel

Axe

Mallet

Marking gauge

Flat bit

Marking out and cutting joints

When working outside cutting swift, basic joints in rough-sawn wood, you need these basic tools: a marking gauge, tenon saw, flat drill bit, chisels, mallet and axe.

A large, single-spike marking gauge is used for setting out the joints on the wood, a tenon saw for removing the bulk of the waste, and a flat drill bit for clearing the mortises. When purchasing the marking gauge, get a good, basic model, which will stand up to wear and tear in the garden.

Once the rough has been cleared from the joint with the saw and drill, you need a selection of bevel-edged chisels for shaving the wood down to the mark. Again, choose good-quality solid chisels. Avoid those with cheap wooden handles that are likely to split, and select tools with solid plastic handles moulded to the shank.

CAUTION

Although chisels and axes are potentially dangerous tools, you can cut the risks to almost zero by always holding the tool with a firm grip, cutting away from your body, and applying full concentration to the job.

For large basic joints we also use a mallet and a small axe. The axe is a particularly useful tool. Apart from all manner of splitting and shaving tasks, such as cutting dowels for pegging joints and trimming the bottoms of posts, the axe can also be used in much the same way as a wide-bladed chisel. A tenon is sawn to the waste side of the shoulder-line, and then the blade of the axe is set on the end-grain mark and driven home with a blow from the mallet. Choose a good, heavy-duty axe, with a thin blade that has a bevel on both sides. Avoid the thick-bladed, stainless-steel axes sold for splitting kindling, opting instead for a hand-forged black iron axe. Pay careful attention to safety considerations when using an axe. Always make sure that your body (and anyone else's) is well clear of the path of swing. Do not use your free hand to hold the wood in position.

TOOLS FOR SCREWING AND NAILING

Drill bit for wood and metal

Electric drill

Cross-point screwdriver

Cordless drill/driver

Claw hammer

Screwing

Before a screw is driven into wood, it is best to drill a pilot hole with a twist drill bit. (In most cases, the holes do not need to be countersunk with a pilot-countersink bit: the pine used for the projects is so soft that the screwhead will cut its own counter-sink.) Then use a variable-speed cordless drill fitted with a cross-point screwdriver bit for driving in the screws. Set the torque on the drill to suit the thickness and hardness of the wood, and drive the screw home until the torque slips the clutch.

Nailing

The projects in this book use slender nails for fixing feather-edged boards to frames, and flat-headed nails for roofing felt. To fix the felt, you simply bang the nails home with a claw hammer. With feather-edged boards, however, you need to drill pilot holes for the nails so that you do not split the fragile grain. Small staples are used for fixing rabbit wire. Make sure that all nails and staples are galvanized. Avoid nails and staples described as "black iron", because they bend and stain the wood.

OTHER ESSENTIAL TOOLS

Metal snips

Adjustable spanner

Sledgehammer

Clamp

Utility knife

Electric sander

Paintbrush

Fixing and finishing

Some projects require a sledgehammer, but don't be tempted to buy the biggest one you can find, because a medium-weight one is more than adequate. When using the sledgehammer, make sure that your helper is standing on the opposite side of the post to be driven home, and that his or her hands are out of harm's way.

Once the woodwork is finished, the project is completed by sanding, painting and preserving. You will need an electric sander for removing large splinters and for sculpting surfaces, a clamp for holding parts together, and a brush for applying paint or preserv-

ative. Depending upon the project, you might also need an adjustable spanner for tightening up nuts, a pair of metal snips for cutting wire mesh, and a utility knife for cutting roofing felt.

If you really need to cut costs on a project, and do not want to go to the expense of kitting yourself out with the tools we have described, see if you can borrow various items from friends and neighbours. You may also want to consider hiring power tools. If you are going to use an unfamiliar tool, it is always a good idea to have a trial run on some scrap wood, just to make sure that you understand how the tool is best handled.

Materials

We obtained all the rough-sawn softwood from a local sawmill, using four types of wood: wood that had been left in its natural state, wood that had been pressure-treated and had a grey-green finish, wood that had been brush-treated to give it a brown finish, and wood described as "short ends and offcut waste".

USEFUL TIMBER SECTIONS

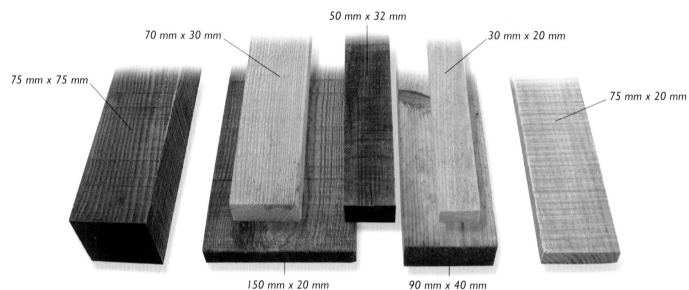

75 mm x 75 mm
70 mm x 30 mm
50 mm x 32 mm
30 mm x 20 mm
75 mm x 20 mm
150 mm x 20 mm
90 mm x 40 mm

Posts, planks and sticks

The sawmill supplied us with rough-sawn softwood intended for garden items such as fences, gates, sheds and screens. We used stick sections ranging from roofing battens about 30 mm wide and 20 mm thick (sold in bundles), through to flat battens 75 mm wide and 20 mm thick (sold to be used for pickets). We purchased posts 75 mm and 100 mm square, planks up to 150 mm wide described as "gravel boards", and all manner of smaller sections.

When you are buying wood, make allowances for inaccuracies in the measurements given by the sawmill. For example, a plank described as being 20 mm thick might actually measure anything from 18 mm through to 23 mm. When you get the wood home, leave it propped up against a wall or fence to dry out for a couple of days, until it feels dry to the touch.

Choosing the right length and section

Most sawmills sell wood in three lengths – 2 m (or 6 ft), 3 m (or 9 ft), and 4 m (or 12 ft). You will need to work out the most economical length for your chosen project. The wood will be sold as square sections, planks, triangular and semicircular rails, grooved decking and cladding. The projects assume that you won't need to cut the wood to a different section size. Be ready to modify the projects to suit the sections sold by your local sawmill. If you are not confident in your ability to adjust the requirements, take your plans to the sawmill and ask for advice.

BUYING TIPS

- Be flexible. If, for example, a project specifies a section 50 mm square, but you are only able to get something 50 mm wide and 25 mm thick, you can screw two sections together.
- Always choose local softwood – it is cheaper and more forest-friendly.
- There are lots of bargains to be had. Go prepared with heavy boots and gloves, and be ready to search through piles of wood that are variously described as trimmings, short ends, offcuts or waney-edged.
- Don't be talked into using imported hardwood or wood that has been overly planed or prepared.
- Remember that while pressure-treated woods are long-lasting, they are also highly toxic (to the extent that your skin might blister on contact). A good option is to buy sawn wood and then treat it with a suitable preservative or paint.
- If you are a woman, be prepared for the fact that most sawmills are run by men and may have a mainly male clientele. Try not to feel intimidated.
- We suggest that you do not take children to the sawmill. But do encourage them to help make the projects, because the planning and building are a good educational experience.

CLADDING

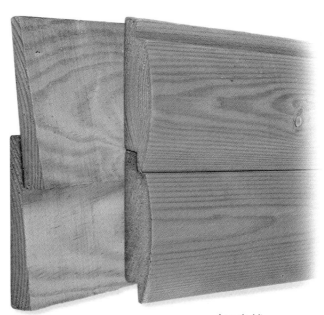

Types of cladding

While we decided to use feather-edged boarding for cladding, most sawmills sell at least two other options. There is ship-lap cladding, which looks a bit like tongue-and-groove boarding, and log cladding, which looks very much like half-logs. In our opinion, the feather-edged cladding is the least expensive, the easiest to work and fit, and the most attractive. The feather edge is also more traditional, and the layering gives a stronger structure.

Nailing feather-edged boards

We always use a jig made from two offcuts screwed together, which is butted against the lower edge of a board to ensure that it overlaps the next one by 35 mm. To avoid splitting the wood, the boards must be drilled prior to fixing, with the holes set so that the nail or screw misses the board that you are just about to lap.

Before fixing the cladding, it is a good idea to have a trial dry run just to make sure that you have enough wood. Arrange each piece so that any knots or splits are clear of the nailing points. When you are driving the nails home, be careful that you do not force the wood to bend into a concave profile, so that it splits.

Log cladding

Feather-edged boarding

OTHER USEFUL SECTIONS AND READY-MADE ITEMS

Ball

Triangular section

Decking

Dowel

Trellis screen

Triangular section and decking

Triangular sections are designed specifically to be used for fence rails. The rails run horizontally from post to post at the back of the fence and are used to support the vertical boards. The widest face of the section is fixed in contact with the fence.

Decking can either be bought in the form of tiles, or by the metre. We purchased our decking in 3 m lengths. We usually avoid buying pressure-treated wood because of its cost and the toxic nature of the preservative, but decking is an exception. Do not let children play on newly-treated timber, to prevent skin coming into contact with the wood. However, decking is subjected to the full blast of the weather, which soon dispenses with the hazard.

Dowels and balls

Dowelling is bought by the metre according to requirements. Finial balls come in all shapes and sizes. Those with a screw attached just need a pilot hole drilling in the post so the ball can be screwed in place. Some balls require a double-ended screw (half the screw goes into the post and the other end into the ball).

Trellis screens

It is possible to make trellis screens from thin lathes, but they are so tricky to make that it is best to purchase them ready-made. Buy your screens before you buy anything else, and then modify all the other measurements to suit.

FIXINGS AND FITTINGS

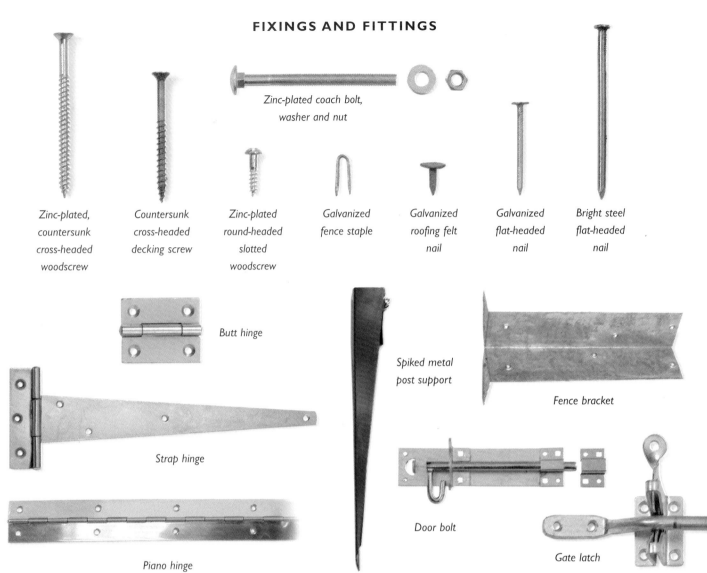

Zinc-plated coach bolt,
washer and nut

Zinc-plated,
countersunk
cross-headed
woodscrew

Countersunk
cross-headed
decking screw

Zinc-plated
round-headed
slotted
woodscrew

Galvanized
fence staple

Galvanized
roofing felt
nail

Galvanized
flat-headed
nail

Bright steel
flat-headed
nail

Butt hinge

Strap hinge

Piano hinge

Spiked metal
post support

Fence bracket

Door bolt

Gate latch

Screws, bolts, nails and staples

We use best-quality, exterior-grade, galvanized or zinc-plated cross-headed screws throughout – because they stay bright and can easily be driven home with a variable-speed, cordless electric drill fitted with a screwdriver bit. Buy boxes of 100 or 200 screws at a time: it is cheaper, and you won't run short of screws.

Coach bolts, with washers and nuts to fit, are used for projects such as the Picket Gate (see page 46). A hole to fit the shank is drilled, the bolt is tapped home until the square section just under the head bites into the hole, and then it is clenched with a washer and nut.

We always buy nails and staples by weight because it is the most cost-effective option. Always specify that they should be galvanized, or at least plated, because then you won't have to worry about rust staining the wood.

Hinges, gate bolts and latches

We use butt door hinges for the Folding Screen (see page 38) and the Rabbit Ark (see page 94), piano hinges for the Children's Playhouse (see page 120), T-strap hinges for the Victorian Tool Shed (see page 108), and heavy-duty reversible hinges for the

Picket Gate (see page 46). The advantage of using piano hinges on a door that children will play with is that the continuous body of the hinge prevents the child from trapping his or her fingers between the door and doorpost. The heavy-duty reversible hinges for the gate are designed to be fixed with both screws and coach bolts, making them even more sturdy.

We also use a latch for the gate and a sliding gate bolt for the tool-shed door. Don't try to cut costs by using cheap metalware. If you have gone to a lot of trouble to build an item, it is a false economy to skimp on the fixings and fittings: always specify that they are galvanized (or at least plated), and always buy the items complete with galvanized bolts and screws to fit.

Post and fence fixings

We use spiked metal post supports for fixing fenceposts and gateposts, because they are very efficient and very easy to fix. The spike is put in position, an offcut is placed on top of the spike, and it is banged home with a sledgehammer. The post is then slid into the containment and held by clamping nuts. The metal fixings for post rails are just as easy to fit. One half is screwed to the triangular-section rail and the other to the post itself.

OTHER MATERIALS

Roofing plywood   *Stirling board*   *Roofing felt*   *Wire mesh*

Plywood, stirling board and felt
To make a board and felt roof, first cover the roof with a sheet of exterior-grade plywood or stirling board. Nail the first sheet of felt in place on the board, paint felt adhesive over the nails, stick the second sheet of felt in place, and so on. The idea is that on the top of the roof at least, the nailed edge of one piece of felt is always covered by the glued edge of the neighbouring piece. It is rather like a tiled roof, where the nailed head end of one tile is covered and protected by the tail end of the neighbouring tile.

Wire mesh and window plastic
We used welded galvanized wire "grid" mesh for the Rabbit Ark (see page 94) rather than woven fence wire, because it keeps its shape and is easier to cut and fit. It is important to buy mesh that is specifically described as being suitable for rabbit cages.

For safety reasons, the window of the Children's Playhouse (see page 120) is glazed with polycarbonate sheet rather than glass. To cut the sheet, score the line of cut with a craft knife – on both sides – and then fold it so that it breaks on the line.

PAINTS, STAINS AND PRESERVATIVES

Red stain/preservative on pine   *Mauve paint/preservative on pine*   *Blue stain/preservative on pine*   *Creosote on pine*

Pressure-treated wood
Pressure-treated wood undoubtedly gives the best protection, but it is both expensive and highly toxic. It is fine for projects such as the Victorian Tool Shed (see page 108) and the Multi-shaped Decking (see page 52), but we wouldn't use it for "close-contact" projects such as the Decorative Picnic Table (see page 56), Rabbit Ark (see page 94) or Children's Playhouse (see page 120). The subject is open to debate, but we would not like a child to sleep in a playhouse made from pressure-treated wood.

Exterior paints and stains
We favour using exterior-grade water-based paint, because the colours can be blended, and the paint can be diluted to give a thin wash or

---

> **CAUTION**
>
> Always wear gloves when you are handling preservatives and paint. Read the labels carefully. If you are worried, take specific advice.

---

stain. We usually colour the wood with a thin wash, and then protect the whole thing with a coat of clear preservative. Always read the labels on the cans and then you will be able to make a value judgement about the best treatment for your project.

Creosote
Creosote oil is smelly and unpleasant to apply, but the rich brown colour is attractive and it does preserve the wood. It is fine for projects such as the Folding Screen (see page 38), but obviously it's a bad idea for the Children's Playhouse (see page 120), Decorative Picnic Table (see page 56) and the Rabbit Ark (see page 94). Many plants wither if they touch wood that has been protected with creosote.

Working with wood

Immersing yourself in creative woodwork outside in the garden is an exciting and therapeutic activity. A pile of sawn sections can be transformed into attractive and useful items, such as a picnic table or tool shed, in the space of a weekend. If you can use a saw and drive in a screw, you are capable of making all the projects in this book.

STRAIGHT CUTS

ABOVE **Use a square for marking 90° cuts. Hold the wooden handle against the edge of the piece of wood and draw a pencil line.**

To make a straight cut (at right angles to the face or edge of the wood), take a square and pencil and mark the wood. Let's say that you want to cut a 600 mm length off a 150 mm-wide plank. Hold the wooden handle (or "stock") of the square hard against the workpiece, and run a pencil line against the edge of the steel blade. Repeat on all faces and edges of the plank, so the line encircles the wood. Clamp the workpiece in a workbench, take a crosscut saw and place the teeth to the waste side of the drawn line. Perform a few short, dragging strokes, and then use the full length of the saw to make the cut. At the end of the cut, use your free hand to support the waste, making lighter strokes until the wood is sawn through.

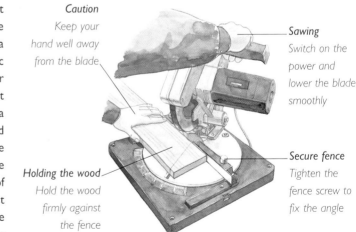

Keeping in line
Keep your whole arm moving in line with the saw and the angle of saw cut

Portable workbench
Make sure the bench is at a comfortable height

Supporting the wood
Use your free hand to support the wood

ABOVE **After marking the length of a piece of wood, use a crosscut saw (for cutting across the grain) to cut it to length. Support the wood on a workbench and saw to the waste side of the pencil line.**

ANGLED CUTS

ABOVE **Use a bevel gauge for drawing angled lines. Set the gauge to the required angle, and use in the same way as a square (shown above).**

To make an angled cut (a straight cut that runs at an angle to the edge of the wood), you can use a crosscut saw or an electric compound mitre saw. For example, imagine that you want to cut an angle across a picket. If are going to use the hand saw, take a bevel gauge, set the angle to suit your needs, hold the handle hard up against the edge of the wood and draw a line against the steel blade. Set the workpiece in the workbench and use the crosscut saw to make the cut as already described. To use the compound mitre saw, first set the blade of the saw to the desired angle and lock it into position. Hold the workpiece hard against the fence, repeatedly lower the blade and nudge the wood until the blade is just to the waste side of the drawn line. Raise the blade, switch on the power, lower the blade and make the cut.

Caution
Keep your hand well away from the blade

Sawing
Switch on the power and lower the blade smoothly

Holding the wood
Hold the wood firmly against the fence

Secure fence
Tighten the fence screw to fix the angle

ABOVE **After marking a straight or angled line, use the compound mitre saw to cut the wood quickly and accurately. The blade can be tilted as well as rotated, so you can also cut compound angles (for example a cut that is 30° across a plank and 20° through it). The saw is especially useful for cutting lots of wood to the same size.**

CUTTING CURVED SHAPES

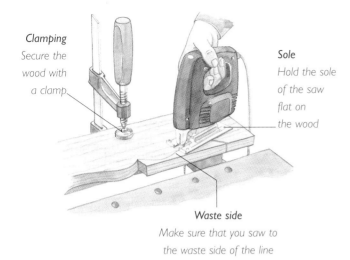

Clamping
Secure the wood with a clamp

Sole
Hold the sole of the saw flat on the wood

Waste side
Make sure that you saw to the waste side of the line

ABOVE The jigsaw is designed for cutting curves in wood. The narrow blade enables the saw to be rotated to follow tight curves in decorative designs. The sole can be locked in a tilted position to produce an angled, curved cut. Always rotate the saw in the direction of a curve rather than forcing the blade sideways.

We use two procedures to draw curved shapes. For shapes that are made of circles and part-circles, we simply use a compass. For symmetrical cyma curves (the ones that look a little like stylized lips) we draw half of the shape freehand, cut it out, and use this as a template to draw the other half. This way of working ensures that the shape is perfectly symmetrical.

To cut curves, you can use either a coping saw for cutting small, tight curves on or near the edge of thin wood, or a power jigsaw for broad curves in thick wood. To use the coping saw, first make sure that the blade is fitted with the teeth pointing away from the handle. Tighten up the blade until it "pings" when plucked. Secure the workpiece in the jaws of a portable workbench, position the blade to the waste side of the drawn line, and work with a steady stroke to make the cut.

To use the power jigsaw, first bridge the workpiece across a couple of workbenches. Set the bed of the saw on the workpiece (so that the blade is just clear of the wood), switch on the power and slowly advance the tool so that the line of cut runs slightly to the waste side of the drawn line. Hold the tool with a firm grip, in order to stop it juddering and vibrating.

CUTTING MORTISE AND TENON JOINTS

Mortise and tenon joints are made up from two mating halves: the mortise (or hole) and the tenon that fits into the hole. The ideal is a joint that is a tight push-fit.

Making procedure to cut a mortise

1 Use a pencil, ruler, square and marking gauge to carefully set out the lines that make up the mortise.
2 Select a drill bit size that fits within the width of the mortise, and bore out one or more holes to clear the bulk of the waste. Hold the drill upright so that the drilled holes are at right angles to the face of the wood. There are various types of mortise. If it is a through mortise (one that goes right through the thickness of the wood), drill the holes completely through. If it is a blind or stopped mortise (the hole doesn't go through the wood), put a piece of masking tape around the drill bit to mark the depth you want to drill to, and stop when the hole reaches that depth.
3 Use a chisel to pare back the sides of the hole to the drawn lines. Work with a series of skimming cuts.

Making procedure to cut a tenon

1 Use a square, rule, pencil and gauge to draw a tenon that is a tight push-fit for the mortise.
2 Secure the workpiece in the portable workbench at an angle of about 45°. Use the saw to cut down to the shoulder-line. Repeat this procedure for both cuts on both sides of the joint.
3 Set the workpiece flat on the bench and saw down to the waste side of the shoulder-line, so that the piece of waste falls away. Do this on both sides of the tenon.

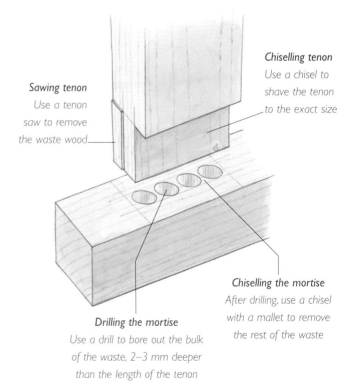

Sawing tenon
Use a tenon saw to remove the waste wood

Chiselling tenon
Use a chisel to shave the tenon to the exact size

Drilling the mortise
Use a drill to bore out the bulk of the waste, 2–3 mm deeper than the length of the tenon

Chiselling the mortise
After drilling, use a chisel with a mallet to remove the rest of the waste

ABOVE The mortise and tenon is a traditional joint for joining two pieces of wood, usually at right angles as shown here. Cut the mortise first with a drill bit and chisel(s), and then cut the tenon with a tenon saw. Mortise and tenon joints are hard work to cut by hand but are often stronger, cheaper and more attractive than fixing with screws or special hardware.

Fences and gates

In the Koran it says, "A fence without a gate is a prison, while a fence with a gate is a paradise". This section shows you how to create your own "paradise" by constructing a fence with an integral gate. Strength and stability are watchwords for both items: they must be able to stand up to both the weather and general wear and tear. Gates must be functional and appropriate for their situation, and should open and close without undue hindrance.

FIXING POSTS

Traditionally, wooden fenceposts and gateposts had half their length set below ground, with the below-ground section first charred or tarred, and then supported with a mix of well-tamped clay and rubble. However, the posts in our projects are best supported with concrete, or with a patent metal post support spike. When digging holes or banging in metal spikes, bear in mind that there may be underground power cables, water and drainage pipes lurking in the earth, so dig cautiously.

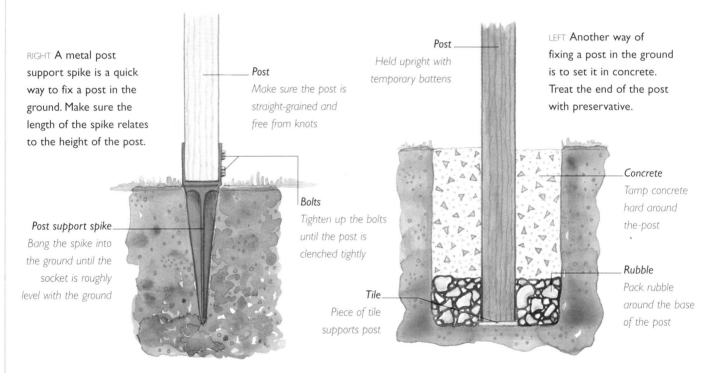

RIGHT A metal post support spike is a quick way to fix a post in the ground. Make sure the length of the spike relates to the height of the post.

Post
Make sure the post is straight-grained and free from knots

Post support spike
Bang the spike into the ground until the socket is roughly level with the ground

Bolts
Tighten up the bolts until the post is clenched tightly

Post
Held upright with temporary battens

LEFT Another way of fixing a post in the ground is to set it in concrete. Treat the end of the post with preservative.

Concrete
Tamp concrete hard around the post

Rubble
Pack rubble around the base of the post

Tile
Piece of tile supports post

Procedure for fixing a post support spike

1 Buy a metal post support spike to suit the length and square section of your post. The taller the post, the longer the length of spike required. Make sure that the spike has a strong bolt-clamp fitting, and that the metal is well protected by being galvanized or painted.
2 Set the support spike on the mark, slide an offcut from your post into the socket at the top of the spike, and give it a little tap with a sledgehammer to insert it just into the ground.
3 Adjust the spike so that it is upright, and bang it down into the ground with the sledgehammer. Continue until the bottom of the socketed top is positioned just above ground level.
4 Finally, set the post in the socket, make adjustments until it is vertical, and clench the bolts with a spanner.

Procedure for fixing a post with concrete

1 Use a spade to dig out a hole about 400 mm deep and 300 mm square. Remove the waste earth from the site.
2 Put a piece of broken tile into the bottom of the hole, position the post on the tile, and tamp a small amount of rubble around the bottom 100 mm of the post.
3 Prop the post upright with three temporary battens (nail the battens near the top of the post and angle them down to make a tripod) and make adjustments until the post is perfectly vertical. Make checks with a spirit level.
4 Make a concrete mix of 1 part Portland cement, 2 parts sharp sand, and 3 parts coarse aggregate (gravel). Tamp it into the hole.
5 Remove the temporary battens after four days. The concrete will not achieve its full strength until about three weeks later.

TYPES OF FENCE

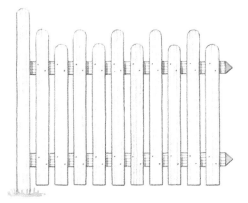

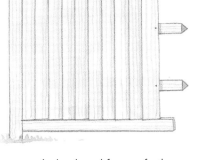

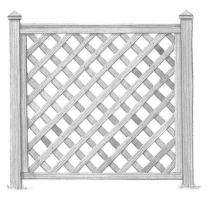

ABOVE A traditional picket fence with rounded ends. The gap between the pickets should be no greater than the width of a picket.

ABOVE A closeboard fence – feather-edged boards framed by the posts, capping rail and bottom board.

ABOVE A diamond trellis (overlapping lathes contained within a batten frame) set between capped posts.

There are various things to take into consideration when planning a fence. Do you need to keep children or livestock in, or wildlife out? Would you like the fence to look attractive and welcoming? Do you want a strong fence that discourages invaders, or a tall fence that prevents prying eyes?

In this book we show you how to make a traditional picket fence (see page 42). The word "picket" comes from the French word *piquer*, meaning "to prick". A picket fence has now come to mean a fence made up from a number of pointed slats; however the word once meant the pointed part of a palisade or wicket. From one country to another, the terms picket, wicket and palisade are more or less interchangeable and loosely used to describe many other types of wooden fence. There are closeboard fences made up from overlapping feather-edged boards, trellis fences made from a woven web of thin sections, and woven willow fences. Ranch-style fences are made from large-section cleft wood, and the rails are dominant; chestnut fences are made from cleft sticks and the posts are dominant.

TYPES OF GATE

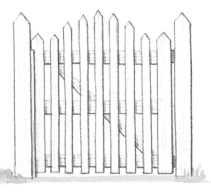

ABOVE A traditional picket gate in an arched pattern, held together with three horizontal rails and a diagonal brace.

ABOVE A gate made from riven wood (split, not sawn) is a good choice for an informal rustic garden. The split wood has a rough texture and varies in width and thickness, giving the gate an unmistakable hand-crafted appearance.

ABOVE Closeboard gates such as this are long-lasting and will prevent pets wandering in and out of your garden.

Gates have much the same history and design variations as fences, but they are more complex structures in that they have additional members such as stiles, braces and posts. Within the basic gate, the vertical side members are called stiles, the horizontal members are called rails, and the diagonal member is called a brace (and of course the gate frame is covered with additional vertical or horizontal members).

The gate is set between two posts – hinged to one and latched to another. Though designs vary, the one constant is that the brace always runs uphill from the hinge side of the gate through to the latch side. If the brace were to be set the other way around, the gate would sag down from the hinge side. A main factor in the strength of a gate is its hinges, and the hinge stile and the hinge post are often built from large-section wood.

Benches, chairs and decking

Every garden needs benches and seats scattered around so that you can enjoy the changing seasons during fine weather throughout the year. If their design includes decorative touches, they are lifted above mere practicality and can become attractive garden features. If your garden is in need of small areas of hard standing, wooden decking is a good-looking solution, which can create a softer effect than stone or concrete.

GARDEN SEATING CONSIDERATIONS

Garden seats must be attractive and well built, and should be positioned to take advantage of sun or shade as required. They can be made to a variety of designs to suit a selection of purposes. We have chosen three different options: a Decorative Picnic Table (see page 56), a Wheeled Bench (see page 68) and a small bench seat set within a Classic Arbour (see page 62). The picnic table can be used for family meals or entertaining. The wheeled bench has been designed for a small garden, incorporating wheels so that it can be moved with ease. It has an integral table, which is a useful place to put a drink. The arbour provides a sheltered spot to sit.

TYPES OF SEATING

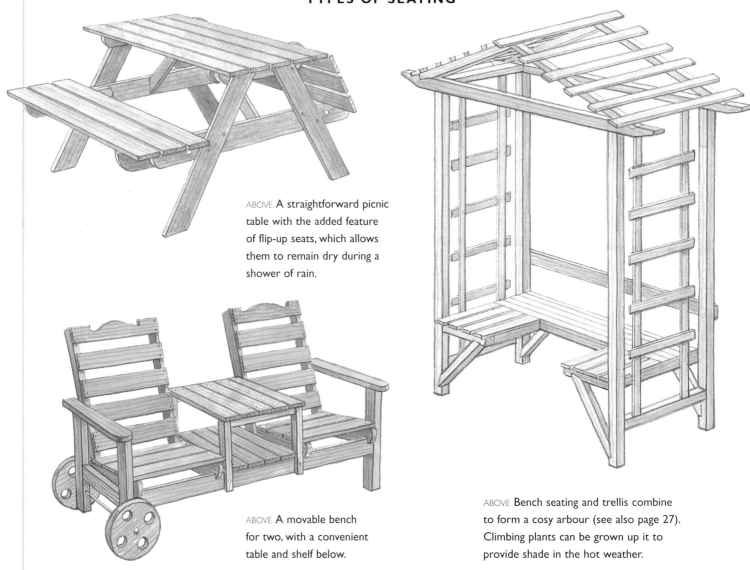

ABOVE A straightforward picnic table with the added feature of flip-up seats, which allows them to remain dry during a shower of rain.

ABOVE A movable bench for two, with a convenient table and shelf below.

ABOVE Bench seating and trellis combine to form a cosy arbour (see also page 27). Climbing plants can be grown up it to provide shade in the hot weather.

TYPES OF CHAIR

ABOVE A traditional painted pine chair with slatted seat and strong mortise and tenon joints.

ABOVE An oriental-style teak chair, ideal for outdoor dining and general use. Heavyweight and long-lasting.

ABOVE A folding chair for occasional use, which can be brought in from the garden during the wet weather.

DECKING

Wooden decking is a great idea for the garden – perfect when you want a level patio without going to all the time, trouble and expense of laying a concrete or stone paved area complete with a massive hardcore and concrete foundation. Furthermore, if you might conceivably want to move the patio from one year to the next, or you have a difficult sloping site, wooden decking is a good contender. There are also aesthetic considerations – perhaps you enjoy the sight and feel of wood – a decked area feels alive and springy, quite different from stone or brick. Also, by building a raised decking, you can achieve an area that gives the impression of a balcony or jetty, which extends and enhances your home.

Procedure for levelling decking

1 Rake the site smooth and cover it with a plastic membrane.
2 Rake a layer of gravel or bark chippings over the plastic, completely covering it to a thickness of about 100 mm.
3 Mark the position of the decking legs on the ground, set each paving slab on a bed of mortar, and wait for the mortar to set.
4 Lift the decking module into position, with each leg resting on a slab. Test to see whether it is level with a spirit level, selecting one leg to become a constant reference point.
5 Make adjustments by adding slabs under one or all of the remaining legs, to make the decking level.

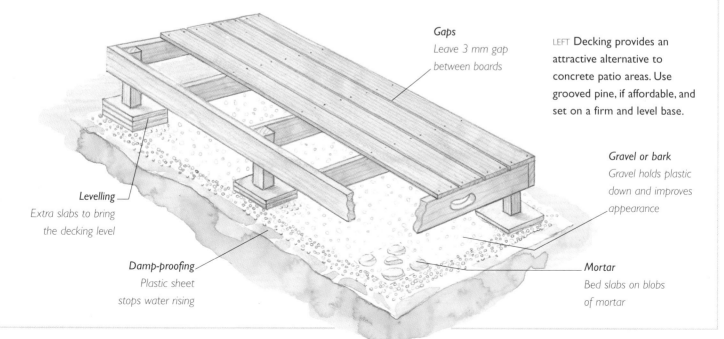

Gaps
Leave 3 mm gap between boards

LEFT Decking provides an attractive alternative to concrete patio areas. Use grooved pine, if affordable, and set on a firm and level base.

Gravel or bark
Gravel holds plastic down and improves appearance

Levelling
Extra slabs to bring the decking level

Damp-proofing
Plastic sheet stops water rising

Mortar
Bed slabs on blobs of mortar

Sheds, houses and arbours

A shed is invaluable for storing all the paraphernalia required for tending the garden. Summerhouses and arbours are beguiling and exciting structures which can enhance a garden, adding texture to the backdrop of plant life. They are functional too, providing a sheltered spot to sit. You can sit and enjoy looking at a cheerful display of bulbs on a fresh spring morning, or appreciate blazing leaf colours on a chilly autumn afternoon.

FOUNDATIONS

All these structures require firm foundations, although you do not necessarily need to go to the trouble of laying a concrete base slab, which involves lots of digging, tamping hardcore, mixing concrete and so on. If the ground is wet and boggy, there is no option other than to lay concrete; otherwise a base made from concrete paving slabs set on a bed of sand is more than adequate.

Procedure for laying a concrete base
1 Skim off the topsoil to a depth of about 100 mm.
2 Position, peg out and level a foundation frame (made from rough-sawn wood 80 mm wide and 25 mm thick).
3 Fill the area within the frame with builder's rubble or a mixture of crushed stone and gravel, to a depth of about 100 mm.
4 Top up the frame with concrete (1 part Portland cement, 2 parts sharp sand, 3 parts aggregate, water); level and tamp with a plank.
5 Remove the wooden frame and rub the sides of the slab with a piece of scrap wood to remove the sharp edges.
6 When dry, lay pads of heavy-duty plastic or felt on the concrete to go under the shed's base bearers.

Procedure for laying concrete slabs
1 Dig away the topsoil to a depth of about 100 mm.
2 Fill the recess with a layer of sharp sand, to a depth of 100 mm, then rake it smooth and level it off.
3 Set the concrete paving slabs on generous wedges of mortar (1 part Portland cement, 6 parts building sand, 1 part hydrated lime, water). Level the first slab with a spirit level and then make sure that all subsequent slabs relate to it.
4 When the mortar has set (two days to harden completely), sit the shed's base bearers on pads of heavy-duty felt or plastic sheet.

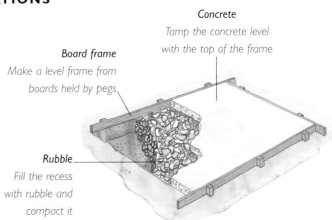

Board frame
Make a level frame from boards held by pegs

Concrete
Tamp the concrete level with the top of the frame

Rubble
Fill the recess with rubble and compact it

ABOVE If the ground is unstable, sheds, garden houses and arbours require a foundation consisting of hardcore and concrete.

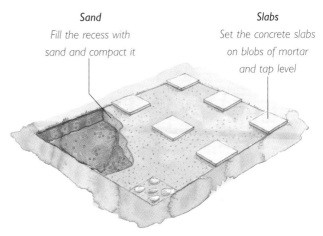

Sand
Fill the recess with sand and compact it

Slabs
Set the concrete slabs on blobs of mortar and tap level

ABOVE Where the ground is stable, paving slabs are an adequate foundation for sheds, arbours and other lightweight structures.

TYPES OF SHED

Sheds are defined and described by the shape of their roof. There are two basic types: the A-frame apex roof, which slopes down from a central ridge board, and the pent roof, which has a single gentle slope. A pent roof is cheaper and easier to build than an apex roof, because it can be made from large sheets of board. When planning a shed, you need to consider the head height required inside the shed, and the way the roof sits in relation to the door. For example, some structures are designed with the slope of the roof running forwards rather than backwards. Certainly the rain drips off at the front, so you get wet going in and out, but on the other hand, the low front prevents driving rain from getting inside the shed.

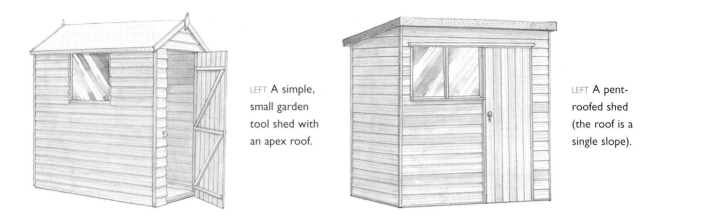

LEFT A simple, small garden tool shed with an apex roof.

LEFT A pent-roofed shed (the roof is a single slope).

SUMMERHOUSES AND OUTDOOR ROOMS

A summerhouse is a retreat, which allows you to get away from your everyday home. It is an opportunity to let your imagination run riot. If you have always harboured fantasies about living in a Wild West cowboy bunkhouse, Swiss cottage or log cabin, your summerhouse is an opportunity to satisfy these urges. Basically, there are two types of summerhouse: the small day room that is just big enough for a couple of chairs and a table, and the room that is large enough to double up as a spare guest room.

ABOVE A Swiss-style summerhouse complete with fancy gable boards, double doors and integral matching window boxes.

ABOVE This Victorian-design octagonal summerhouse has arched windows and a roof vent.

ABOVE An elaborate summerhouse with a lovely verandah, thistle-pattern banister rails and decorative woodwork on the gable.

ARBOURS

Generally speaking, an arbour is no more than a roof supported on poles – an open-sided structure that is just about big enough for a couple of seats. Arbours are very similar to gazebos in that they are often used to support scented climbing plants such as honeysuckle. Our Classic Arbour (see page 62) has a solid back and a waterproof roof, the idea being that it can be built in a small garden and pushed up against a wall or fence to be used as a bower, rather like a miniature summerhouse.

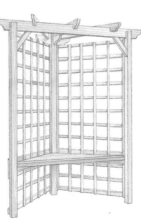

LEFT An arched arbour in an American design of the early nineteenth century.

LEFT A corner arbour with pergola beams and trellis sides.

LEFT A Victorian-style arbour with plenty of ornate details.

Pergolas, trellises and planters

If you want to add an eye-catching feature to your garden, you will find this section useful. Pergolas and trellises provide a support for plants and add a vertical dimension to the geography of the garden. If you would like to create stunning seasonal displays of flowers, our two patio planters (see pages 34 and 82) provide solutions.

TYPES OF PERGOLA

A pergola is best defined as a pattern of beams supported by a collection of posts, rather like a basic hut frame. In essence, there are four types of pergola design. A traditional rustic frame is made from poles cut straight from the tree and nailed together. A straightforward pergola is made from sawn square sections notched and screwed together. A slightly more elaborate variation on this has the ends of the crossbeams shaped and profiled. Finally, a lean-to pergola is designed to be built up against a wall.

The rustic pergola is exciting to build, but the actual jointing is made more difficult by the fact that the sections are round. Our design for the Classic Pergola (see page 100) is something of a hybrid, with the cross beams made by laminating pairs of planks.

Whatever the design, the structure must be strong and stable enough to withstand high winds. The best way to do this is to fix it with screws, wait for the structure to settle, and then run galvanized bolts through the primary joints.

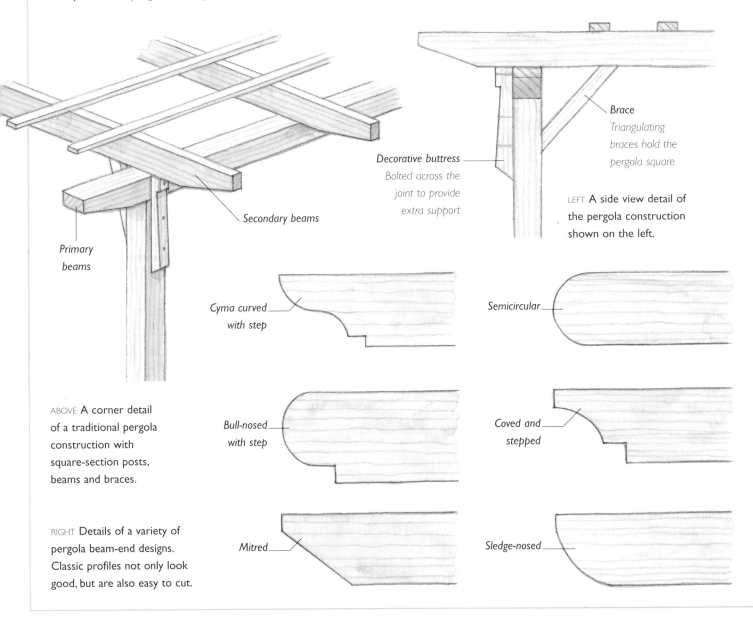

Secondary beams

Primary beams

ABOVE A corner detail of a traditional pergola construction with square-section posts, beams and braces.

RIGHT Details of a variety of pergola beam-end designs. Classic profiles not only look good, but are also easy to cut.

Decorative buttress
Bolted across the joint to provide extra support

Brace
Triangulating braces hold the pergola square

LEFT A side view detail of the pergola construction shown on the left.

Cyma curved with step

Semicircular

Bull-nosed with step

Coved and stepped

Mitred

Sledge-nosed

TRELLISES

Trellises are traditionally made from sawn lathes arranged in a square or diamond grid pattern. The trellis is either contained within a frame or fixed to a stronger support, and then mounted on a wall, used as a space filler between two posts, or fixed between a wall and a post.

Naked trellis can be used as an effective design motif, but it is mostly used as a support for climbing plants. If you want to use trellis as a plant support, make sure, when purchasing, that it has been treated with a plant-friendly preservative. Some trellises are painted with toxic preservatives that kill plants on contact. Perhaps the most attractive type of trellis is one described as "riven", which means that the lathes are split rather than sawn, giving the structure a curvy appearance. The highest quality of trellis you can buy is made by hand from riven hardwood such as oak or hazel, and the intersections are fixed with bent and clenched copper nails.

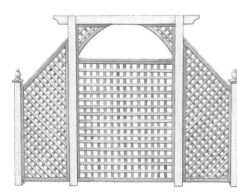

ABOVE A Victorian patio trellis with neo-Japanese beam design. Trellises of this type were traditionally used as freestanding backdrop features at the end of walkways.

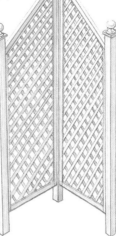

ABOVE Book-fold trellis – this is designed to be used in a corner area.

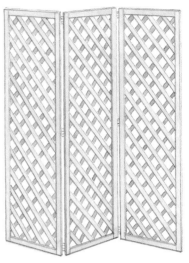

ABOVE A traditional folding trellis: this can also be used in a conservatory.

PLANTERS

Planters are best defined as self-contained plant-holders. The plants within it have no contact with the ground underlying the planter. Some planters hold earth, but our Corner Patio Planter (see page 82) is designed as a repository for a number of potted plants. Position it on your patio, balcony, or conservatory. The air space underneath the planter ensures that the structure remains sound and free from rot. When individual plants have passed their best, or you would simply like a change, remove or add plants as desired. The Tiered Patio Planter project (see page 34) gives you the opportunity to create a really dramatic display.

ABOVE A planter with integral trellis and finial posts is a stylish structure.

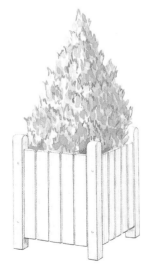

ABOVE A traditional English design – usually displayed in pairs by a doorway.

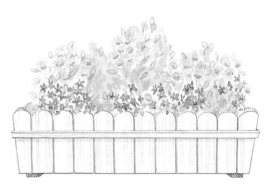

ABOVE Pickets are adaptable components, which can be used for constructing various planters. Small ones are suitable for window boxes; larger versions are good for grander patio containers.

Finishing

In the context of garden woodwork, the term "finishing" has very little to do with bringing the surface of the wood to a smooth, shiny finish – as you would do when building fine furniture. Rather, it is the procedure of finishing a project by ensuring a satisfactory colour and surface texture, which is suitably protected or preserved.

SANDING

Sanding or rubbing down is the process of using sandpaper to smooth wood to a textural finish that suits your requirements. The degree of sanding is a matter of personal choice. For example, while you might want to sand the handles and arms of the Wheeled Bench (see page 68) to a really butter-smooth finish,

you might well do no more than remove large splinters from the sides of the Classic Arbour (see page 62). We employ a power sander because it is so quick and easy to use. When fitted with a coarse sandpaper, it is possible to sculpt wood to shape – as shown by the handles of the Rabbit Ark (see page 94).

APPLYING PAINTS, STAINS AND PRESERVATIVES

RIGHT Deciding how to paint and/or preserve garden woodwork is not always straightforward. Bright colours, although appealing, may be too dominant in your garden, particularly in winter, so choose carefully. Always read the directions for applying paint and preservative and wear protective gloves.

Colour
Use exterior paint over a clear preservative, or choose a product that preserves and colours in one go

Application
For speed, use brush sizes that relate to the size of area you are painting – smelly preservatives can be applied using a brush fixed to the end of a stick

Preserving
Most exterior woodwork should be painted with preservative

Colourwashing
Colourwashing is the technique of diluting a water-based paint with water, and painting the resulting wash over the wood. This can then be rubbed through in places if desired, to reveal the underlying wood. We like this finish for many reasons – it is possible to mix an unlimited range of subtle colours, it is very cheap, it is non-toxic, and the finish blends in with nature. When choosing your paints, make sure that they are the water-based type specifically designed for exterior use.

Painting
Unlike interior painting, where you nearly always need to sand wood to a smooth finish first, or the exterior painting of woodwork such as doors and windows, for which spirit-based gloss paints are mostly used, painting garden woodwork involves very little sanding and is done with water-based paints. All we do is rub down the wood to remove the worst of the splinters

and then brush on the paint. The more textured the wood, and the thicker the paint, the more exciting and dynamic the finish achieved. When the paint is dry, we favour rubbing though areas of paint to create a worn and weathered appearance.

Preserving
Not so long ago, the only product for preserving garden wood-work was dark brown creosote, but now there are many other options. You can buy wood that has been pre-treated with a clear or coloured preservative, or apply a preservative yourself. Alternatively, you can paint the wood and then give the item a coat of clear preserva-tive. For structures such as gates and fencing, which you do not come into close contact with, a good coat of creosote takes a bit of beating. But for items such as tables and benches, and particularly the Children's Playhouse (see page 120), you must ensure that a non-toxic preservative is used.

> **USEFUL TIP**
>
> If you want to avoid using paints and preservatives altogether, opt for a long-lasting wood such as Western red cedar.

Maintenance

Maintenance is the procedure of keeping garden woodwork in good order and fit for its intended purpose. Every autumn and spring, make sure that fixings are firm and have not rusted, check that wood is sound, and apply paint or preservative if necessary. You will then be able to enjoy your wooden items for many years to come.

REPAIRING AND REPLACING

Repairing and replacing

The forces of nature and normal wear and tear mean that garden woodwork is under constant attack. Metal may rust, wood may go mouldy, or structures may break from misuse. If you want your projects to last for more than a couple of seasons, you do need to spend time repairing and replacing fixings that are less than sound.

You will need to oil hinges and latches, make sure screws are free from rust, replace pieces of rotten or broken wood, renew torn or pierced roof felt, add more bolts, and so on. The best time to do these tasks is in the early spring (after the wind and rain of winter and before the peak garden season of summer) and then again in the autumn (after a summer's use and before the winter). By following this routine conscientiously, you can expect most of the projects to last for up to ten years.

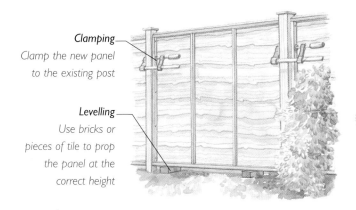

Clamping
Clamp the new panel to the existing post

Levelling
Use bricks or pieces of tile to prop the panel at the correct height

ABOVE Replacing a damaged fence panel. Fences made from thin wood, resembling this one, will need regular maintenance.

Procedure for mending a fence panel

1 Remove dying foliage and tie plants back so that you are able to move freely around the fence panel. Discuss the situation with your neighbour if it is a boundary fence.
2 Remove the broken panel along with any clips or fixings, and make sure that both posts are sound and in good order. Give the posts a generous coat of a suitable preservative.
3 Take your replacement panel and position it between the two posts. Check the level and make height adjustments by standing the panel on bricks or tiles.
4 Clamp the panel in place. Drill holes from the edge of the panel through into the post and fix with galvanized screws.

Procedure for mending feather-edged cladding

1 Wedge the overlapping board out of the way, and use a pair of long-nosed pliers or a wire cutter to snip the nails or screws so that the damaged piece of wood falls away.
2 Buy a length of feather-edged board to match the damaged piece and cut it to fit.
3 Ease the new board up under the overlapping board and use a clamp to hold it in place. Remove the wedge.
4 Drill pilot holes through the new board and its underlying piece and fix in place with galvanized screws.

Procedure for mending a felt roof

1 Cut around the hole in the roof and remove the damaged felt, together with any accumulated grit and debris.
2 Daub a generous amount of felt adhesive in and around the hole and let it dry completely.
3 Daub more adhesive over the first layer, then stick a patch of new felt over the damage and fix with flat-headed galvanized nails.
4 Finally, stick a larger patch of felt over the first patch, which covers all the nail heads with a generous overlap.

Fixing
Glue and nail the first patch and then glue the top patch over the first

Ladder
A board under the ladder stops it sinking into the ground

ABOVE Felt roofs can suffer after a bout of hot or severe weather. The double-patch procedure avoids nailing through the exposed felt.

Part 2: **Projects**

Tiered patio planter

If you have ever stared enviously at the stunning displays of flowers exhibited at professional flower shows, and wondered how the designers manage to achieve such beautiful cascading tiers of blooms, this project tells you how. To create a similar effect, you need to display flowers on a purpose-built tiered planter.

EXPLODED VIEW OF THE TIERED PATIO PLANTER

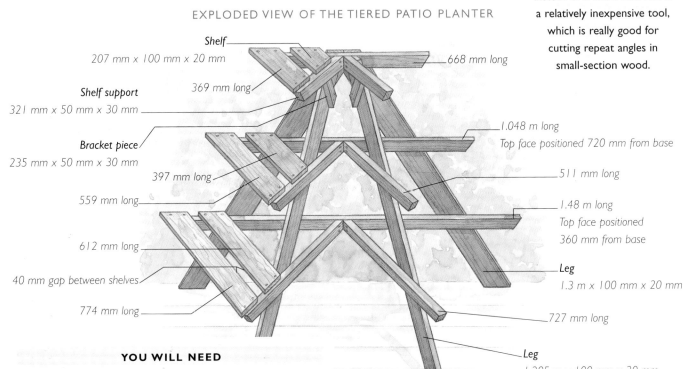

Shelf
207 mm x 100 mm x 20 mm

668 mm long

Shelf support
321 mm x 50 mm x 30 mm

369 mm long

Bracket piece
235 mm x 50 mm x 30 mm

397 mm long

559 mm long

612 mm long

40 mm gap between shelves

774 mm long

1.048 m long
Top face positioned 720 mm from base

511 mm long

1.48 m long
Top face positioned 360 mm from base

Leg
1.3 m x 100 mm x 20 mm

727 mm long

Leg
1.285 m x 100 mm x 20 mm

YOU WILL NEED

Materials *for a planter 1.1 m high, 1.5 m wide and 690 mm deep. (All rough-sawn pine pieces include excess length for wastage.)*
- Pine: 7 pieces, each 3 m long, 100 mm wide and 20 mm thick (shelves, legs and braces)
- Pine: 6 pieces, each 2 m long, 50 mm wide and 30 mm thick (shelf supports)
- Zinc-plated, countersunk cross-headed screws: 100 x 38 mm no. 8, 50 x 50 mm no. 10,
- Acrylic paint, colour to suit
- Clear preservative

Tools
- Pencil, ruler, tape measure, marking gauge and square
- Portable workbench and G-clamp
- Plywood workboard about 1 m square
- Crosscut saw
- Cordless electric drill with a cross-point screwdriver bit
- Drill bits to match the screw sizes
- Electric compound mitre saw
- Electric sander with a pack of medium-grade sandpaper
- Paintbrush: 40 mm

A HIGH-RISE DISPLAY

This planter is designed to be pushed against a wall, with the flowers being viewed from the front. However, the height of the stand and the fact that it is based on a hexagon also mean that the display will be cone-like in form – so if you were to arrange 50 potted plants on it, you would see a towering hill of blooms.

The tiered shelves enable you to design a display where the focus is directed towards the plants rather than their pots. We have painted the wood a rich red colour, so that when there are gaps in the display and the supporting skeleton peeks through, it looks attractive. The structure stands well over a metre high, but even so, the splay of the legs allows it to be fully loaded without any danger of it tipping forward.

Because you are likely to be watering the plants daily, we have given the wood extra protection by sealing the paint with a coat of clear preservative. You may prefer to go for a brown colour rather than the red we have used, but do not use a high-odour preservative such as creosote, because the plants will not like it.

Step-by-step: Making the tiered patio planter

Workboard
*Square the top support
with the workboard*

Screwholes
*Drill holes for the screws to
avoid splitting the wood*

*Parallel
supports*
*Make sure
that the three
shelf supports
are parallel to
one another*

Cordless driver
*Charge the
driver the
day before
you start
the project*

Supports
*Butt the
supports
together so
that they
meet on the
centre-line*

1 Take the two legs that make the primary back frame and centre them on top of the three primary shelf supports. Butt the legs together at the top, check the angles and squareness, and drive 38 mm screws through into the legs.

2 Turn the back frame over so that the shelf supports are uppermost, and screw the secondary supports in place with 50 mm screws – so that they angle out at 60° from the centre. Take care: the structure is fragile at this stage.

3 Set the secondary legs in place, so that they meet at top centre, and screw them to the side of the supports with one 38 mm screw at each intersection. Check the angles and positioning and then drive in the second screws.

Screwing
*Position the
screws to
avoid knots*

Helpful hint

If you find that the whole structure is difficult to support while you work, you could either ask a friend to help or secure the various components with clamps.

Power cable
Make sure the power
cable is clear of the saw

Screw position
Make sure you do not put a screw
close to the end of the support

Caution
Switch off the
power before
moving the
workpiece

Shelf centre
Align the ends
of the shelves
with the
centre-line of
the supports

Shelf position
Butt the
shelves
together on
the centre-line

4 Clamp the electric compound mitre saw on the portable workbench, check that it is stable, and set the machine to cut at an angle of 60°. Cut all the shelves to length.

5 Starting at the bottom tier and working upwards, set the shelf boards in place on the supports, with the butted ends of the shelves meeting the centre-line of the supports. Screw in place with 38 mm screws.

6 Fix the two bracket pieces in place in the angle on the underside of the top shelf, using 50 mm screws. Finally, rub down the wood to remove the splinters, give it a thin wash of acrylic paint and brush on the clear preservative.

Screwdriver
You might need
to use a hand
screwdriver at
this stage if
your cordless
driver is too big

Angled support
Drive the screw
home so that
the bracket is a
tight fit

Folding screen

A folding screen is a very useful item for the garden. It can be used to create a separate space or "room", which might be used for relaxing, or for a dining area, or even for a children's play corner. If you yearn for somewhere to sneak off to and read a book, find a nice quiet part of the garden or yard, preferably by lots of flowers or a favourite plant, and site the screen so that you have your own private space. Even greater privacy is available if you clothe the screen in climbing plants.

TIME

Two long days' work (most of the time for building the screen, and about an hour to get it sited).

USEFUL TIP

If you decide to open the screen wider than 90°, it will need to be secured with pegs or spiked post supports.

YOU WILL NEED

Materials *for a screen 1.174 m square and 2.289 m high. (All rough-sawn pine pieces include excess length for wastage.)*

- Pine: 4 pieces, each 3 m long and 70 mm square (main posts)
- Pine: 4 pieces, each 2 m long and 70 mm square (main horizontal rails)
- Ready-made pine trellis screens: 2 screens, 1.86 m high and 930 mm wide
- Pine dowel: 8 pieces of 10 mm dowel, each 70 mm long (for pegging the joints)
- Pine turned balls: 4 balls with screws to fit (post finials)
- Galvanized steel fence panel U-clips: 12 with screws to fit
- Galvanized steel large butt door hinges: 2 with screws to fit
- Clear preservative

Tools

- Pencil, ruler, tape measure, marking gauge and square
- Portable workbench
- Mallet
- Bevel-edged chisel, 30 mm wide
- Crosscut saw
- Small axe
- Claw hammer
- Electric drill with a 10 mm flat bit
- Cordless electric drill with a cross-point screwdriver bit
- Drill bits to match the screw sizes
- Electric sander with a pack of medium-grade sandpaper
- Paintbrush: 40 mm

EXPLODED VIEW OF THE FOLDING SCREEN

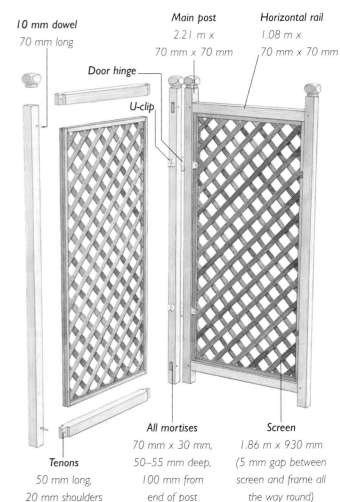

10 mm dowel
70 mm long

Door hinge

U-clip

Main post
2.21 m x
70 mm x 70 mm

Horizontal rail
1.08 m x
70 mm x 70 mm

Tenons
50 mm long,
20 mm shoulders

All mortises
70 mm x 30 mm,
50–55 mm deep,
100 mm from
end of post

Screen
1.86 m x 930 mm
(5 mm gap between
screen and frame all
the way round)

A COSY, QUIET CORNER

The folding screen is portable, but it is not terribly easy to move, so the idea is that it is installed in the garden in the spring, and stored away in the winter. The way it folds allows you to set it up at an angle that is greater than 90°.

You may decide to use the screen as a permanent feature, for example as a backdrop for a wall mask fountain, with the lattice being employed to disguise the workings of the fountain. Alternatively, it could become a support for a vine or other climbing plant. In either case, the feet need to be held secure in spiked post supports for safety. The frame is held together with tenons on the ends of the rails and mortises in the posts. The ready-made trellis screens are fitted with panel U-clips. The shop-bought ball finials are simply screwed into the top of the posts.

Because we chose to use contrasting materials for this project – brown-stained trellis screens and natural finish posts – we decided to protect the wood with a clear preservative to retain the freshness of the colour contrast.

Step-by-step: **Making the folding screen**

Mallet size
Choose a solid mallet with a square-faced head

On target
Make sure the mallet hits the axe head and not the handle

Chisel grip
Hold the chisel firmly and keep it upright

Grain
If the wood is not straight-grained, use a saw rather than the axe

1 Set out the blind mortises on all four main posts – 100 mm along from the ends, 30 mm wide and 70 mm long – and chop them out with the mallet and chisel. Aim to cut the mortises slightly over 50 mm deep.

2 Set out the tenons on the ends of all four main horizontal rails, making them 50 mm long and 30 mm wide, with 20 mm-wide shoulders to the sides. Next, saw down to the waste side of the shoulder-line, then clear the waste wood using the axe and chisel.

Hole alignment
Align the holes and gently tap the dowel into place (avoid hitting it too hard, which may damage the dowel or the frame)

3 Knock the joint together, then drill a 10 mm hole right through the joint and peg it with a length of dowel. Screw the finial balls in place.

Helpful hint

If you damage a dowel while knocking it into the hole – or the dowel breaks off – use a hammer with a screwdriver to drive the dowel through the joint and out the other side. Check that the drilled hole is big enough for the dowel before trying again.

Equal gap
Maintain a 5 mm gap between
trellis and frame all the way round

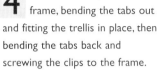

4 Screw six U-clips on each frame, bending the tabs out and fitting the trellis in place, then bending the tabs back and screwing the clips to the frame.

Trellis
The best
trellis is either
stapled or
nailed at the
intersections

U-clips
Choose
galvanized clips
made from thin
metal, which is
easy to bend

Alignment
Make sure
that the two
frames are
perfectly
aligned before
you screw the
hinges on

5 Position the two frames side by side and on edge so that the spine posts are uppermost. Screw the hinges in place (you can either recess the hinges or surface-mount them). Finally, rub down the screen with sandpaper and lay on a coat of clear preservative.

Hinge position
Position the
hinges to
avoid knots

Picket fence

White-painted picket fences conjure up images of country cottages and flower-filled gardens. If you are fed up with your mass-produced garden fence – whether it is ungainly chicken wire or ugly concrete blocks – a picket fence is an attractive solution. (See also the Picket Gate project on page 46.)

(See also the Picket Gate project on page 46.)

| **TIME** |
| A day for every 2-metre length of fence. |

| **USEFUL TIP** |
| You can adjust the height of the pickets to suit your own requirements. |

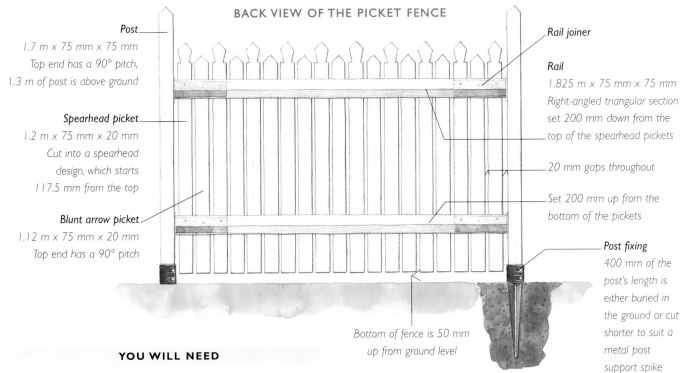

BACK VIEW OF THE PICKET FENCE

Post
1.7 m x 75 mm x 75 mm
Top end has a 90° pitch,
1.3 m of post is above ground

Spearhead picket
1.2 m x 75 mm x 20 mm
Cut into a spearhead
design, which starts
117.5 mm from the top

Blunt arrow picket
1.12 m x 75 mm x 20 mm
Top end has a 90° pitch

Rail joiner

Rail
1.825 m x 75 mm x 75 mm
Right-angled triangular section
set 200 mm down from the
top of the spearhead pickets

20 mm gaps throughout

Set 200 mm up from the
bottom of the pickets

Post fixing
400 mm of the
post's length is
either buried in
the ground or cut
shorter to suit a
metal post
support spike

Bottom of fence is 50 mm
up from ground level

YOU WILL NEED

Materials *for a fence 1.975 m long and 1.3 m high. (All rough-sawn pine pieces include excess length for wastage.)*

- Pine: 10 pieces, each 3 m long, 75 mm wide and 20 mm thick (spearhead pickets and blunt arrow pickets)
- Pine: 2 pieces 75 x 75 mm right-angled triangular section, each 2 m long (rails)
- Pine: 1 piece, 2 m long, 30 mm wide and 20 mm thick (temporary batten)
- Pine: 2 pieces, each 2 m long and 75 mm square (posts)
- Zinc-plated, countersunk cross-headed screws: 200 x 38 mm no. 8

- Galvanized steel rail joiners: 4 to suit your rail size and section
- Matt white exterior-quality paint

Tools
- Pencil, ruler, tape measure, bevel gauge and square
- Crosscut saw
- Two portable workbenches
- Cordless electric drill with a cross-point screwdriver bit
- Drill bit to match the screw size
- Electric sander with a pack of medium-grade sandpaper
- Paintbrush: 40 mm

A COUNTRY COTTAGE FENCE

The fence is made up from two picket designs: the blunt arrows have a finished length of 1.12 m and the spearheads reach 1.2 m. The posts are 1.7 m long, with 400 mm of this set in the ground. The bottom of the fence is positioned about 50 mm up from ground level. The top rail is set 200 mm down from the top of the spearheads, while the bottom rail is set 200 mm up from the bottom of the pickets. We have allowed 50 mm on the length of each picket for cutting waste.

In many ways, this is a kit fence, with the rail and the rail joiners as standard; however the design of the pickets is most certainly something that you can chop and change to suit your own needs. The rails are triangular in cross-section, with the short sides measuring about 75 x 75 mm and the hypotenuse 100 mm. When you come to putting the fence together, the pickets are screwed to the 100 mm face of the rails, the galvanized joiner plates are screwed to the ends of the rails, and the flaps of the joiners are screwed to the posts. Finally, the fence is sanded to remove splinters and painted white.

Step-by-step: Making the picket fence

First picket
Screw the first
picket 20 mm
along from the
end of the rails

Triangular jig
Use scraps of
triangular
section to
make a cradle
for each rail

1 Cut the pickets as described on page 48. Lay the two triangular rails on the workbenches (so that they are parallel and 600 mm apart) and screw a spearhead picket in position 20 mm along from each end of the rail. Screw the temporary batten to the bottom ends of the pickets.

Spacer
Set a picket
on edge as
a spacer

2 Using a picket as a spacer, screw the pickets in place so that their ends butt up against the temporary batten. Continue until you have used up all the pickets. Saw the rails to length.

Helpful hint

Stagger the positioning of the screws on each picket – one towards the top of the rail, the other towards the bottom. This avoids splitting the wood. Remember that the rails are triangular, so do not screw near their edges, otherwise the screw will break out of the wood.

Pilot holes
Run pilot holes through the plate holes and into the wood

Drill angle
Hold the drill so that the bit is at 90° to the plate

3 Screw the galvanized joiner plates in position on the triangular rails so that the flaps are flush with the cut ends. Be careful, because the edges of the plates are sharp.

Alignment
Align the face of the flaps with the end of the rail

Angled top
Make two 45° cuts to create the 90° pitched top

Picket pattern
The shoulders of the spearhead pickets should align with the corners of the blunt arrow pickets

Screw angle
Run the screw in at a slight angle so that it avoids the edge of the post

Rail joiner
The joiner becomes stronger when all the screws are in position

Saw cut
Start the saw cut with several strokes pulling towards you

4 Take the two posts and set out the top ends with a 90° pitch. Saw off the waste and use the sander to give the sawn faces a quick rub-down – just enough to remove the splinters and rough edges.

5 Align the fence with the posts (so that the joiner plate flaps are aligned with the back edge of the post) and screw it into position. Fix the posts as described on page 49. Finally, sand off the splinters and paint the whole fence white.

Picket gate

Of all the projects in the book, the picket gate is, at one and the same time, one of the prettiest, easiest to build, and most eye-catching. If you are looking to create a garden with the appeal of a traditional cottage plot, which will be complemented by a little gate that invites opening, this is the project for you. The gate can, of course, be incorporated into the Picket Fence project on page 42.

be incorporated into the Picket Fence project on page 42.

> ### TIME
> A weekend (a long day for building the gate and a day to get it into position).

> ### USEFUL TIP
> Don't be tempted to cut costs on the hinges: they need to be heavy-duty and galvanized.

YOU WILL NEED

Materials *for a gate 995 mm wide and 1.3 m high. (All rough-sawn pine pieces include excess length for wastage.)*
- Pine: 9 pieces, each 1.185 m long, 75 mm wide and 20 mm thick (spearhead pickets)
- Pine: 1 piece, 3 m long, 100 mm wide and 20 mm thick (horizontal rails and diagonal brace)
- Pine: 2 pieces, each 2 m long and 75 mm square (gateposts)
- Pine: 1 piece, 2 m long, 30 mm square (gate stop)
- Painted steel post support spikes: 2 complete with bolts (to support the gateposts)
- Heavy-duty, galvanized steel reversible strap hinges: 2 with screws and coach bolts to fit
- Galvanized steel latch: 1 with screws to fit

- Zinc-plated, countersunk cross-headed screws:
  100 x 38 mm no. 8
  50 x 50 mm no. 8
- Matt white exterior-quality paint

Tools
- Pencil, ruler, tape measure, bevel gauge and square
- Portable workbench
- Plywood workboard about 1.5 m square
- Jigsaw
- Cordless electric drill with a cross-point screwdriver bit
- Drill bits to match the screw sizes
- Crosscut saw
- Sledgehammer
- Spanner to fit your chosen coach bolts
- Electric sander with a pack of medium-grade sandpaper
- Paintbrush: 40 mm

BACK VIEW OF THE PICKET GATE

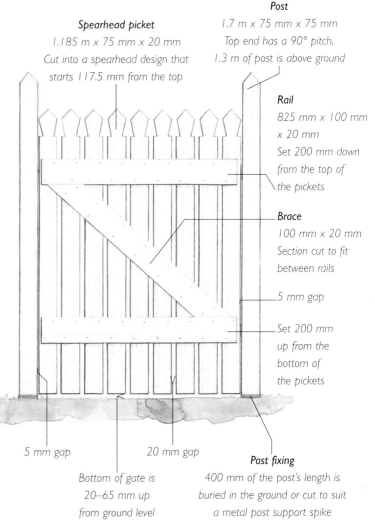

Spearhead picket
1.185 m x 75 mm x 20 mm
Cut into a spearhead design that starts 117.5 mm from the top

Post
1.7 m x 75 mm x 75 mm
Top end has a 90° pitch, 1.3 m of post is above ground

Rail
825 mm x 100 mm x 20 mm
Set 200 mm down from the top of the pickets

Brace
100 mm x 20 mm
Section cut to fit between rails

5 mm gap

Set 200 mm up from the bottom of the pickets

5 mm gap

20 mm gap

Bottom of gate is 20–65 mm up from ground level

Post fixing
400 mm of the post's length is buried in the ground or cut to suit a metal post support spike

PICTUREBOOK PICKET GATE

Although the gate is designed to complement the picket fence, we have varied the design slightly by using spearhead pickets throughout. You do not have to follow suit, but this shows that it is possible to change the emphasis of the design simply by opting for one arrangement of pickets rather than another.

The 75 mm-wide pickets are spaced 20 mm apart and screwed to the 100 mm-wide horizontal rails, and then the arrangement is braced with a single diagonal. Note how the brace – with this gate or any gate – is always fitted so that the bottom end is on the hinge side, and also how the rails are cut slightly shorter than the total width of the gate. We opted for using the post support spikes for three good reasons. Not only are they wonderfully easy to fit – you just bang them in and the job is done, but they instantly make the posts firm, and the whole operation can be managed without the need to mess up the site by digging holes. The gate is naturally quite strong, but the galvanized strap hinges greatly increase its strength, because the screws and coach bolts clench the layers together tightly.

Step-by-step: **Making the picket gate**

First cut
Cut inwards from the
side first

Clamp
Secure the
workpiece with
a clamp

Jigsaw
Cut to the
waste side of
the drawn line

1 Take the 1.185 m-long pickets
and set out the spearheads
with 90° tops. Position the
shoulders 117.5 mm down. Fret
out the shape with the jigsaw.

Right angles
Make sure that
the rails cross
the pickets at
right angles

2 Place the spearhead pickets
on the workboard, cross
them with the horizontal rails,
check the alignment and spacing,
and fix with two 38 mm screws
at each crossover intersection.

Helpful hint

To double-check that the
gate is square, you can use
the workboard (which
should be square) as a
guide. First drive in one
screw at each joint, align
the gate with a corner of
the workboard (pushing it
into a square shape if
needed) and then drive in
the second lot of screws.

Angled joint
Butt the diagonal hard
up against the rail

3 Using the crosscut saw, cut the diagonal brace to length so that it fits the diagonal. Trim the ends to fit the angles, and then butt it in place and fix with 38 mm screws. Use two screws for each intersection.

Screwing
Use two screws
to fix each
picket to the
diagonal brace

Adjustments
You may need
to make
adjustments to
the angle on
the ends of the
diagonal brace

Post offcut
Put a post offcut in the post support spike
while you are hitting it into the ground

Hinge type
Use heavyweight
galvanized hinges

Bolt position
Position the
spike so that
you will be
able to reach
the bolt

Coach bolt
The square
shank of the
bolt should be
a tight fit in
the square
hinge hole

Gate height
Use a scrap of
wood to prop
up the gate at
the correct
height

4 Cut the two gateposts to shape as shown on page 45. Use the sledgehammer to bang the two post support spikes into place so that they are flush with the ground. Trim the bottom of the posts to fit and bolt them in position.

5 Rub down the gate and gateposts with the sander and paint them white. Hang the gate in position, complete with strap hinges and latch. Using 50 mm screws, fix the gate stop to the catch post and paint it white.

Inspirations: Decorative gates

Garden gates hint at what lies beyond them. A gate needs to be functional, but it should also express a message. It might say, "Please come in", "Welcome", or perhaps "This part of the garden is a haven, the perfect place to sit and ponder." The design can be straightforward and inexpensive to realize, or you may prefer to embellish your garden with a customized design that makes use of more expensive varieties of wood and carefully crafted details.

ABOVE A beautiful oak gate complete with finials, lapped and pegged joints, chamfered details and forged iron strap hinges. Its artistic appearance complements the formal clipped hedges that border it and suggests an interesting garden beyond.

LEFT A simple picket gate is the perfect partner for this pretty country garden. It is low in height, strong enough to keep children and pets in, and above all it is welcoming. If you want to make an inexpensive gate, this is a good type to choose.

ABOVE A beautifully constructed gate, with vertical square-section staves contained within a simple frame. Each rail is made from two components that have been cut, stepped and bolted together to sandwich the staves.

Multi-shaped decking

If your garden is the focus for an ever-changing programme of activities – an area for the children to play and a place for hosting family barbecues or entertaining friends, all of which would benefit from a hard standing – our super modular decking is a good option. The decking can be shaped to suit your needs.

YOU WILL NEED

Materials *for 3 decking shapes 1 m wide and 2 m long. (All rough-sawn pine pieces include excess length for wastage.)*
- Pine: 6 pieces, each 2 m long, 150 mm wide and 20 mm thick (long side frame boards)
- Pine: 5 pieces, each 3 m long, 150 mm wide and 20 mm thick (short end frame boards and dividing support planks)
- Pine: 24 pieces, each 3 m long, 95 mm wide and 18 mm thick (grooved decking)
- Pine: 4 pieces, each 2 m long and 100 mm square (legs)
- Zinc-plated, countersunk cross-headed screws: 200 x 38 mm no. 8, 100 x 50 mm no. 10

- Green acrylic paint
- Clear preservative

Tools
- Pencil, ruler, tape measure, compass, bevel gauge and square
- Two portable workbenches
- Crosscut saw
- Electric drill with a 50 mm-diameter saw-toothed cutter to fit
- Electric jigsaw
- Cordless electric drill and cross-point screwdriver bit
- Drill bits to match screws
- Electric compound mitre saw
- Electric sander with a pack of medium-grade sandpaper
- Paintbrush: 40 mm

HIGH AND DRY AND SITTING COMFORTABLY

This is, without doubt, one of the simplest projects in the book. In essence, it is no more than three frames (each the size of a single bed), which are clad with grooved decking boards. Each frame is made up from six 200 mm-long legs, with the four side boards and three dividing boards all put together in such a way that the finished frame makes a module precisely 1 m wide and 2 m long. The idea of the decking is that the three frames can variously be fitted end to end, side by side, end to side, or in any combination to create a surface that always measures a number of whole metres in width and depth. The spacing of the grooved decking allows good airflow, and the handle holes make it easy to lift.

The middle legs are centred on the long side frame board; the middle dividing support plank is screwed to one side of the middle leg, with the other two dividing planks set to quarter the total length. We painted the side and end frame boards green, but you might prefer a natural finish or perhaps a more startling colour.

EXPLODED VIEW OF THE MULTI-SHAPED DECKING

Decking board
45° ends cut from 95 mm x 18 mm grooved pine section

Short end frame board
1 m x 150 mm x 20 mm

Handle hole
100 mm long and 50 mm wide

Long side frame board
1.96 m x 150 mm x 20 mm

Dividing support plank
960 mm x 150 mm x 20 mm

Leg
200 mm x 100 mm x 100 mm

Step-by-step: Making the multi-shaped decking

Saw-toothed cutter
Hold the drill perfectly upright

Clamping
You may want to use a clamp to hold the board still

Spacer
Use a spare piece of 20 mm-thick board as a spacer to help you position the leg

Flush fit
Slide the leg down until the top is flush with the board

Waste board
Put a piece of waste board under the hole to be drilled

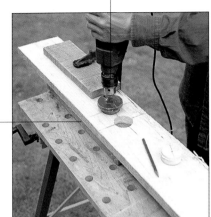

1 Use the crosscut saw to cut the short end frame boards to size (1 m long). Draw out the handle holes, making them 100 mm long and 50 mm wide, and clear the waste with the electric drill and saw-toothed cutter, and the jigsaw.

2 Cut the 100 mm-square wood for the legs into eighteen 200 mm lengths – one for each leg. Set two legs 20 mm in from the ends of the short end frame boards, check that they are square and fix them with 50 mm screws.

3 Cut the long side frame boards to a length of 1.96 m and fix the middle leg in position with 50 mm screws. Butt the end of each board in place on the side of the corner legs and hard up against the inside face of the short end frame board, and fix with 50 mm screws.

Middle leg
Position the leg halfway along the board

Helpful hint

Search out a level area of lawn to work on. Ask a friend to help hold the frame upright while you work, or clamp the frame to a workbench.

Clamping
Clamp the end of the frame in the jaws of the vice

Divider position
Screw the middle divider to one side of the leg

4 Bridge the frame across the two workbenches and fix the three 960 mm-long dividing support planks in place. Screw the middle divider to the legs with 38 mm screws, and fix the quarter dividers with 50 mm screws running through the long side board.

Screw fixing
Locate the divider by screwing through the long side frame boards and into the end of the divider

Screws
Use two 38 mm screws at each end of the lengths of decking

5 Set the electric compound mitre saw to an angle of 45° and set to work cutting the decking to length. Cut the longest boards first and fill in the corners with the various offcuts. Sand all the boards. Paint the long side frame and short end frame boards green. Seal the completed decking module with a coat of clear preservative.

Screws
Use one or two 38 mm screws at the points where the decking crosses the dividing support planks

Decorative picnic table

There is something really enjoyable about eating outdoors. There are fewer worries about etiquette or spillages when you gather to eat around a picnic table, guaranteeing that any meal is a relaxed affair. The beauty of this table is that it can live outside all year, and doesn't have to be dragged out and assembled to make the most of a sunny day in spring, summer or winter.

TIME

A long day's work (about six hours for the woodwork, and the rest of the time for putting together and finishing).

USEFUL TIP

Avoid wood that has been pressure-treated with strong-smelling, toxic preserving fluid. Go for a low-odour, water-based finish.

YOU WILL NEED

Materials *for a picnic table 1.625 m wide, 1.826 m deep and 720 mm high. (All rough-sawn pine pieces include excess length for wastage.)*
- Pine: 12 pieces, each 2 m long, 150 mm wide and 22 mm thick (tabletop and seat boards; cross supports)
- Pine: 2 pieces, each 2 m long, 100 mm wide and 50 mm thick (legs)
- Pine: 4 pieces, each 2 m long, 75 mm wide and 20 mm thick (diagonal braces and cross tie boards)
- Galvanized coach bolts: 16 bolts, 85 mm long, with 16 nuts and washers to fit
- Zinc-plated, countersunk screws: 100 x 38 mm no. 8 100 x 50 mm no. 8
- Clear preservative

Tools
- Pencil, ruler, tape measure, compass, bevel gauge and square
- Two portable workbenches
- Crosscut saw
- Large clamp
- Electric jigsaw
- Plywood workboard about 1 m square
- Spanner to fit the nuts
- Cordless electric drill with a cross-point screwdriver bit
- Drill bits to match the screw sizes, bolt holes and decorative holes
- Electric sander with a pack of medium-grade sandpaper
- Paintbrush: 40 mm

PICNIC TIME

This table is strong, sturdy, decorative and can seat up to eight. It's longer and wider than most tables, with a central hole for a sun umbrella, and lots of curves and curlicues to make it attractive and user-friendly. We have rounded off all the corners so people will not scrape their shins. The frame is clenched with lots of coach bolts, so it stands absolutely firm. We went out of our way to use boards pre-treated with a water-based, non-toxic preservative: this is vital for a surface where food will be served. We chose to use sawn timber, because we like the texture, but rubbed down all edges and surfaces to a smooth, non-splintering finish.

EXPLODED DETAIL OF THE DECORATIVE PICNIC TABLE

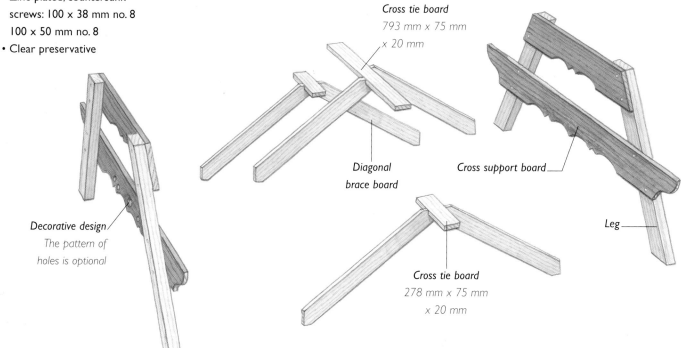

Cross tie board
793 mm x 75 mm x 20 mm

Diagonal brace board

Cross support board

Leg

Cross tie board
278 mm x 75 mm x 20 mm

Decorative design
The pattern of holes is optional

Decorative picnic table

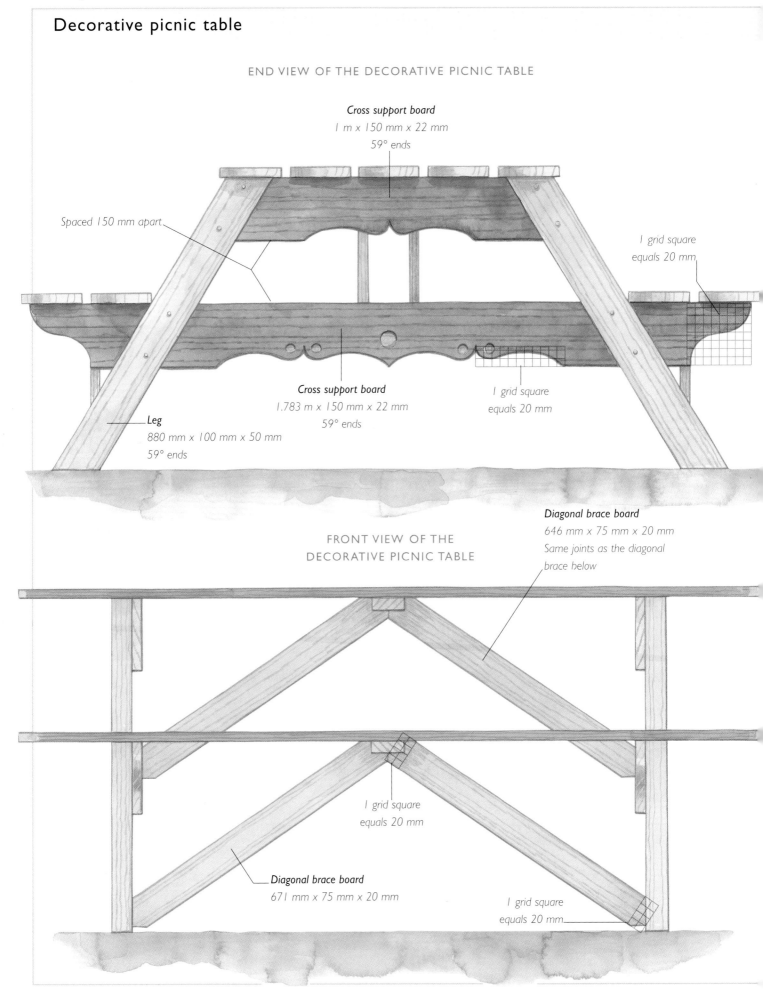

 END VIEW OF THE DECORATIVE PICNIC TABLE

Cross support board
1 m x 150 mm x 22 mm
59° ends

Spaced 150 mm apart

1 grid square
equals 20 mm

Cross support board
1.783 m x 150 mm x 22 mm
59° ends

1 grid square
equals 20 mm

Leg
880 mm x 100 mm x 50 mm
59° ends

Diagonal brace board
646 mm x 75 mm x 20 mm
Same joints as the diagonal
brace below

FRONT VIEW OF THE
DECORATIVE PICNIC TABLE

1 grid square
equals 20 mm

Diagonal brace board
671 mm x 75 mm x 20 mm

1 grid square
equals 20 mm

PLAN VIEW OF THE DECORATIVE PICNIC TABLE

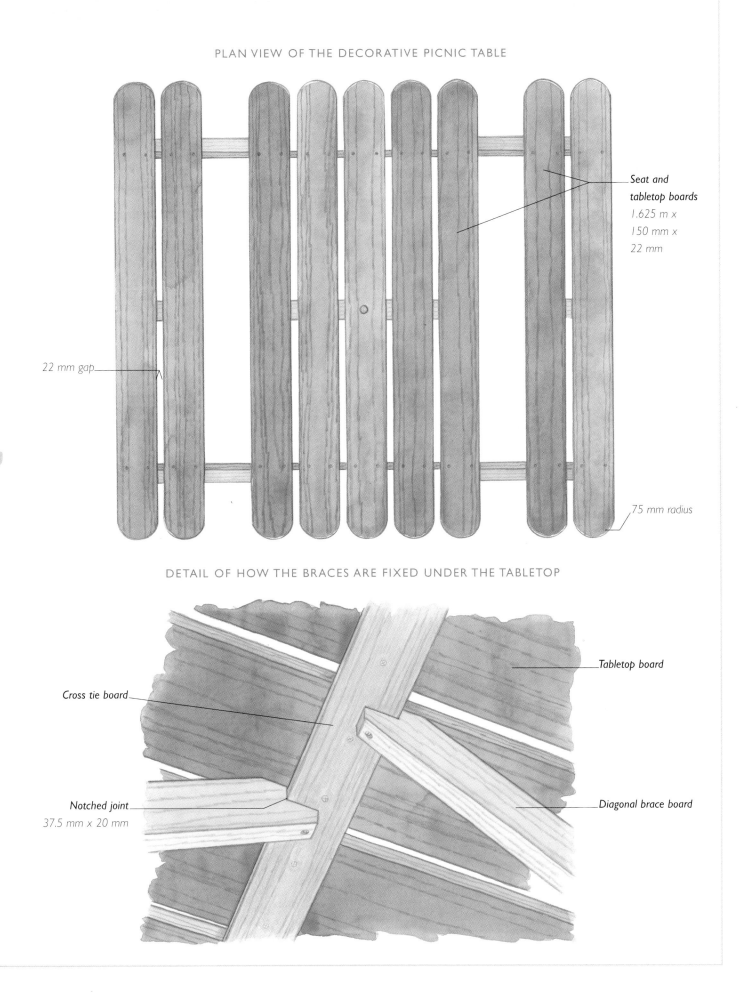

Seat and
tabletop boards
*1.625 m x
150 mm x
22 mm*

22 mm gap

75 mm radius

DETAIL OF HOW THE BRACES ARE FIXED UNDER THE TABLETOP

Tabletop board

Cross tie board

Notched joint
37.5 mm x 20 mm

Diagonal brace board

Step-by-step: **Making the decorative picnic table**

Cutting the curves
Rotate the saw in the direction of the cut, rather than forcing it sideways

1 Cut the boards to length with the crosscut saw and draw out the imagery. Clamp each workpiece to the workbench and fret out the curves with the jigsaw. Work from side to centre in order to achieve a crisp central cleft.

Clamp position
Put the handle of the clamp under the bench so that it does not get in your way

Board position
Set up the board so that the area to be cut hangs over the bench

2 Set the plywood workboard flat on the ground to support the components, and carefully bolt the legs and the cross supports together. Check the arrangement with a square. Note how the components have been spaced with the aid of a 150 mm-wide board.

Hole size
Check that the hole is large enough for the bolt to pass through easily

Board spacer
Use an offcut of 150 mm-wide board as a spacer

Diagonals
If the diagonal measurements are identical, the table is square

Central hole position
Keep all the screws well away from the centre

Seat board
Butt the seat board against the side of the angled leg

Screws
Avoid driving the screws below the surface of the wood as they may break through on the other side

Cross tie board
The cross tie board needs to be positioned centrally and squarely

3 Link the legs by screwing the two outer seat boards in place with a single 50 mm screw at each joint. Ease the frame until its squareness is confirmed by identical diagonal measurements, and then drive in the other 50 mm screws. Screw all the other seat and tabletop boards in place with 50 mm screws.

4 Screw a cross tie board in place across the underside of the tabletop, using 38 mm screws, with the screws positioned well clear of the actual centre-point, and then bore out a hole for the sun umbrella. Screw the diagonal braces in place with 50 mm screws.

Notched braces
All the braces align with the edge of a plank

5 With 38 mm screws, fix the cross tie boards under the seat boards, and then cut and notch the two diagonal braces so that they butt joint at the centre. Screw the brace boards in place with 50 mm screws. Sand the table to a splinter-free finish and brush on the preservative.

Helpful hint

If you are having trouble fitting the notched braces accurately – maybe the ones you have cut are too long – keep trimming the end of one until it fits perfectly, and then use this as a template for cutting the opposite brace.

Classic arbour

An arbour is not only a practical idea (a perfect way of providing a sheltered seat), but a beautiful and decorative structure in its own right. With climbing plants grown up its sides, particularly scented varieties such as jasmine and honeysuckle, you can create a delightful nook to escape to. Use it as a quiet place to read a book, or make it a corner for a romantic rendezvous – it's up to you.

YOU WILL NEED

Materials *for an arbour 1.492 m wide, 1.114 m deep and 2.738 m high. (All rough-sawn pine pieces include excess length for wastage.)*

• Lattice screens: 4 screens, 1.83 m x 303 mm (sides)
• Pine: 4 pieces, each 2 m long, 75 x 75 mm square section (main posts)
• Pine: 15 pieces, each 3 m long, 50 mm wide and 32 mm thick (roof and back panels, seat supports and A-brace)
• Pine: 6 pieces, each 3 m long, 150 mm wide and 22 mm thick (top and bottom side boards, seat, decorative barge boards)
• Pine feather-edged board: 20 pieces, each 3 m long, 100 mm wide and 10 mm thick (back panel and roof)

• Zinc-plated countersunk cross-headed screws: 100 x 50 mm no. 8, 100 x 60 mm no. 10, 20 x 89 mm no. 10
• Galvanized wire nails: 1 kg 40 mm x 2.65 mm
• Clear preservative

Tools

• Pencil, ruler, tape measure, compass, bevel gauge and square
• Two portable workbenches
• Cordless electric drill with a cross-point screwdriver bit
• Selection of drill bits to match screw sizes
• Crosscut saw
• Hammer
• Four large clamps
• Electric jigsaw
• Electric sander with a pack of medium-grade sandpaper
• Paintbrush: 40 mm

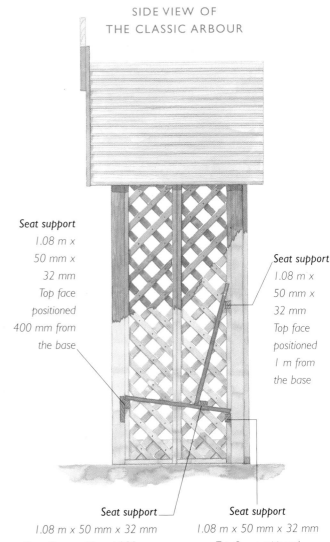

SIDE VIEW OF THE CLASSIC ARBOUR

Seat support 1.08 m x 50 mm x 32 mm Top face positioned 400 mm from the base

Seat support 1.08 m x 50 mm x 32 mm Top face positioned 1 m from the base

Seat support 1.08 m x 50 mm x 32 mm Front face positioned 200 mm from the back of the seat planks

Seat support 1.08 m x 50 mm x 32 mm Top face positioned 300 mm from the base

CONTEMPLATIVE SEAT FOR TWO

This project is built around four slender lattice screens. Buy the screens first, as you may only be able to obtain them in a slightly different size to that we have quoted, and make adjustments to other materials if necessary. Basically, the arbour is a seat for two enclosed on three sides, with a roof over the top. We have designed the project so that it can be made as six knockdown units – the two lattice sides, the back panel, the two roof panels and the seat – with various other pieces used to support and decorate. The feather-edged boards are lapped in such a way that they channel rain off the roof and back panel. The strength and

stability of the overall structure are guaranteed by diagonal braces fixed to both the back panel and the roof. When we went to purchase the materials, the only available lattice screens and 150 mm boards were pre-treated with rather heavy brown wood preservative, so we decided to lift the design by leaving all the other components in their natural colour.

Classic arbour

EXPLODED VIEW OF THE CLASSIC ARBOUR

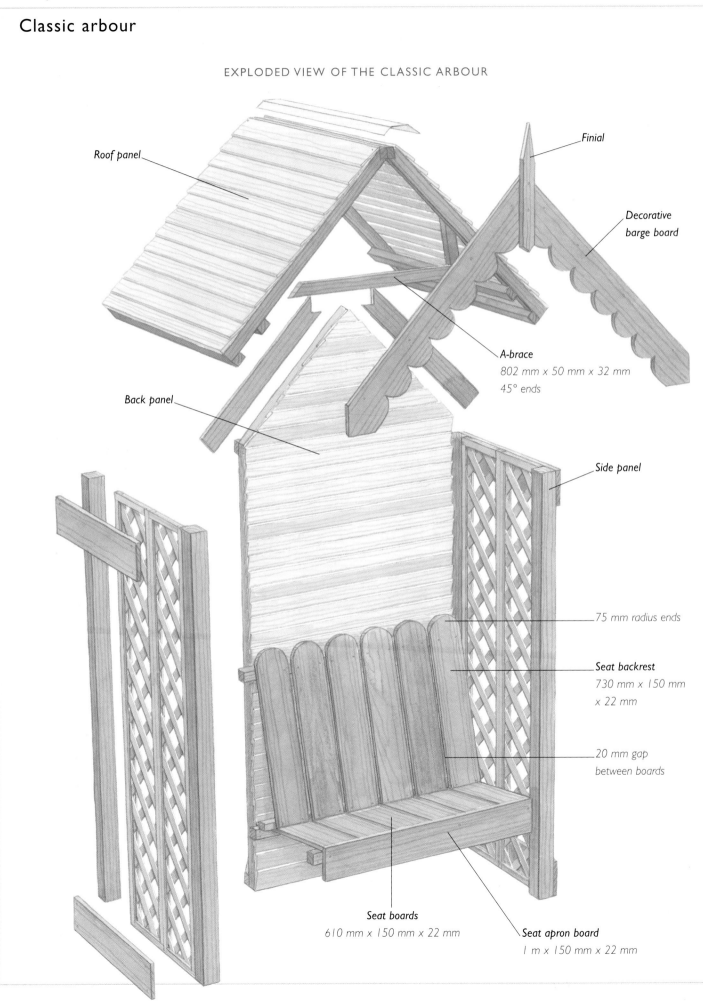

Roof panel

Finial

Decorative
barge board

A-brace
802 mm x 50 mm x 32 mm
45° ends

Back panel

Side panel

75 mm radius ends

Seat backrest
730 mm x 150 mm
x 22 mm

20 mm gap
between boards

Seat boards
610 mm x 150 mm x 22 mm

Seat apron board
1 m x 150 mm x 22 mm

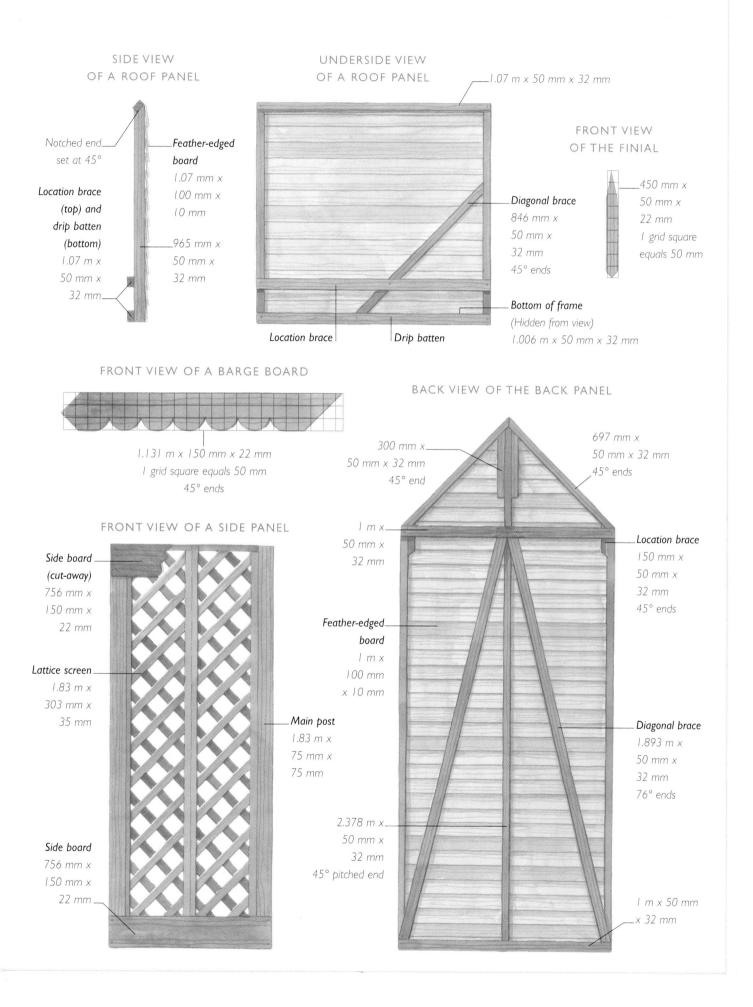

SIDE VIEW
OF A ROOF PANEL

Notched end
set at 45°

Location brace
(top) and
drip batten
(bottom)
1.07 m x
50 mm x
32 mm

Feather-edged
board
1.07 mm x
100 mm x
10 mm

965 mm x
50 mm x
32 mm

UNDERSIDE VIEW
OF A ROOF PANEL

1.07 m x 50 mm x 32 mm

Diagonal brace
846 mm x
50 mm x
32 mm
45° ends

Location brace

Drip batten

Bottom of frame
(Hidden from view)
1.006 m x 50 mm x 32 mm

FRONT VIEW
OF THE FINIAL

450 mm x
50 mm x
22 mm
1 grid square
equals 50 mm

FRONT VIEW OF A BARGE BOARD

1.131 m x 150 mm x 22 mm
1 grid square equals 50 mm
45° ends

FRONT VIEW OF A SIDE PANEL

Side board
(cut-away)
756 mm x
150 mm x
22 mm

Lattice screen
1.83 m x
303 mm x
35 mm

Main post
1.83 m x
75 mm x
75 mm

Side board
756 mm x
150 mm x
22 mm

BACK VIEW OF THE BACK PANEL

300 mm x
50 mm x 32 mm
45° end

697 mm x
50 mm x 32 mm
45° ends

1 m x
50 mm x
32 mm

Location brace
150 mm x
50 mm x
32 mm
45° ends

Feather-edged
board
1 m x
100 mm
x 10 mm

Diagonal brace
1.893 m x
50 mm x
32 mm
76° ends

2.378 m x
50 mm x
32 mm
45° pitched end

1 m x 50 mm
x 32 mm

Step-by-step: **Making the classic arbour**

Screwing
*Drive the screws through
the side of the lattice*

Lattice
*Arrange the
two screens
side by side
so that the
pattern is
aligned*

1 Sandwich the lattice screens between the main posts and screw them in place with 50 mm screws. Set a 150 mm-wide board at top and bottom and screw these to the posts with 50 mm screws. Re-run this procedure so that you have two identical side panels.

Block joints
*Pre-drill the blocks to
prevent splitting*

Strengthening
*Use long
offcuts to
strengthen the
ridge joint*

2 Use the 50 mm x 32 mm section to make the back frame. Cut the parts to size with the crosscut saw and fix them with 60 mm screws. Screw blocks of waste at the angles to help firm up the joints.

Nailing
*Use one nail at each end
of the board*

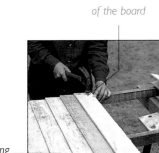

Overlapping
*Make sure that
the boards are
overlapped in
the correct way*

3 Cut the feather-edged board into 1 m lengths and position these on the back frame so that they lap over from top to bottom, ensuring that rain will be thrown off the back of the arbour. Drill pilot holes and fix the strips to the frame with the 40 mm nails.

Feather-edged board
*The boards are lapped so that water
runs off the back of the arbour*

Clamping
*Set the clamps
so that they
are away from
screw positions*

4 Clamp the two side panels to the back panel and fix with the 60 mm screws. Drive the screws through the edges of the panel and into the posts. Check the structure for squareness and then add the additional horizontal and diagonal braces to the back panel.

Seat support
*The planks that form the seat backrest
are fixed to two battens*

Location brace
*The brace locates the roof on the posts
and needs to be positioned accurately*

Drip batten
*Drill holes for
the screws
when you are
working near
the end of a
piece of wood*

Sanding
*Sand the
seat boards
to remove
sharp corners
and splinters*

Diagonal brace
*The diagonal
brace is used
to set the roof
panel square*

5 Position and fit the base for the seat, and then build off the seat to make the backrest. Fit the seat support battens with 50 mm screws. Use the jigsaw to cut the 75 mm radius curves on the top of the backrest boards. Leave a 20 mm space between the boards on both the seat and the backrest.

6 Build and clad the two roof panels in much the same way as the back panel, and then fix additional strengtheners in place with 60 mm screws – a diagonal brace, a drip batten, and a location brace (see the working drawing).

Location
*Centre the location brace
on top of the post*

Positioning
*Set the top edge of the barge board so
that it is higher than the roof strips*

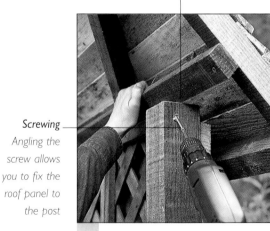

Screwing
*Angling the
screw allows
you to fix the
roof panel to
the post*

Clamping
*Use a clamp to
hold the board
in postion while
you work*

A-brace
*This horizontal
bar prevents
the roof from
spreading*

7 Set the two roof panels in place, so that the location batten is more or less centred on the post (at all four corners) and fix with the 89 mm screws. Run the screws up at an angle, with at least two screws for each post.

8 With 50 mm screws, fix the A-brace to link the two roof panels. Draw the shape of the barge boards and fret them out with the jigsaw. Clamp the boards in place and fix with 50 mm screws. Fit the finial spike to cover the joint. Finally, sand everything to a splinter-free finish and give the arbour a coat of preservative.

Wheeled bench

Imagine going out into the garden on a beautiful morning to sit and enjoy the sunshine. Unfortunately, as soon as the sun moves, you will be left shivering in the shade. However, if you were sitting on our beautiful wheeled bench, you would simply take hold of its handles and move it to a sunny location.

YOU WILL NEED

Materials *for a bench 1.898 m wide, 775 mm deep and 877 mm high. (All rough-sawn pine pieces include excess length for wastage.)*

• Pine: 3 pieces, each 3 m long, 90 mm wide and 40 mm thick (main handle beams, legs, stretchers, axle blocks)
• Pine: 2 pieces, each 2 m long, 150 mm wide and 20 mm thick (arms and shaped backrest boards)
• Pine: 2 pieces, each 3 m long, 50 mm wide and 30 mm thick (table supports, table front horizontal, back rail)
• Pine: 8 pieces, each 3 m long, 100 mm wide and 20 mm thick (seat slats, back slats and tabletop)
• Pine: 4 pieces, each 2 m long, 75 mm wide and 20 mm deep (seat and back supports)
• Pine: 1 piece, 2 m long, 40 mm wide and 20 mm thick (underarm supports)
• Plastic wheels: 2 wheels, 200 mm in diameter, 20 mm holes in centres
• Galvanized threaded rod: 1 m long and 20 mm in diameter (size to suit wheel holes), with 6 washers and 6 nuts to fit
• Zinc-plated, countersunk screws:
  100 x 48 mm no. 8,
  100 x 70 mm no. 10

• Matt green acrylic paint
• Clear preservative

Tools

• Pencil, ruler, tape measure and square
• Portable workbench
• Crosscut saw
• Cordless electric drill with a cross-point screwdriver bit
• Drill bits to match the screw sizes
• Electric jigsaw
• Electric sander with a pack of medium-grade sandpaper
• Electric drill with a 20 mm flat bit and a 10 mm twist bit
• Spanner to fit the nuts
• Paintbrush: 40 mm

A SEAT IN THE SUN

This bench is built with butt joints throughout. There are no complex saw cuts to make or expensive fixings to buy – the bench is created by lots of straight cuts and put together with a generous number of screws. However, the strength of the main joints (where all the 90 x 40 mm sections come together at the corners) relies on the joints being tight. Therefore it is vital that all your measurements and saw cuts are as accurate as possible.

Note how at all the important structural intersections, for example where the legs pass through the frame, the screws are always run into strong face grain, rather than into weak end grain. While the components that make up the main frame are square to each other, the seat and back supports are, for reasons of comfort, canted back at a slight angle. The bottoms of the legs on the wheel side of the bench are reduced in height by 15 mm and the corners chamfered to allow the bench to be tilted up and pushed along. We painted the finished bench with a wash of green acrylic paint, and when it was dry rubbed it down to cut through the paint on edges and corners. The whole bench was then given a coat of clear preservative.

SIDE VIEW OF
WHEELED BENCH

Underarm support
500 mm x 40 mm x 20 mm

Seat support
Raised 40 mm from the top of the front beam (the back support is tilted so that the corner coincides with the top inside corner of the handle rail)

Wheeled bench

EXPLODED VIEW OF THE WHEELED BENCH

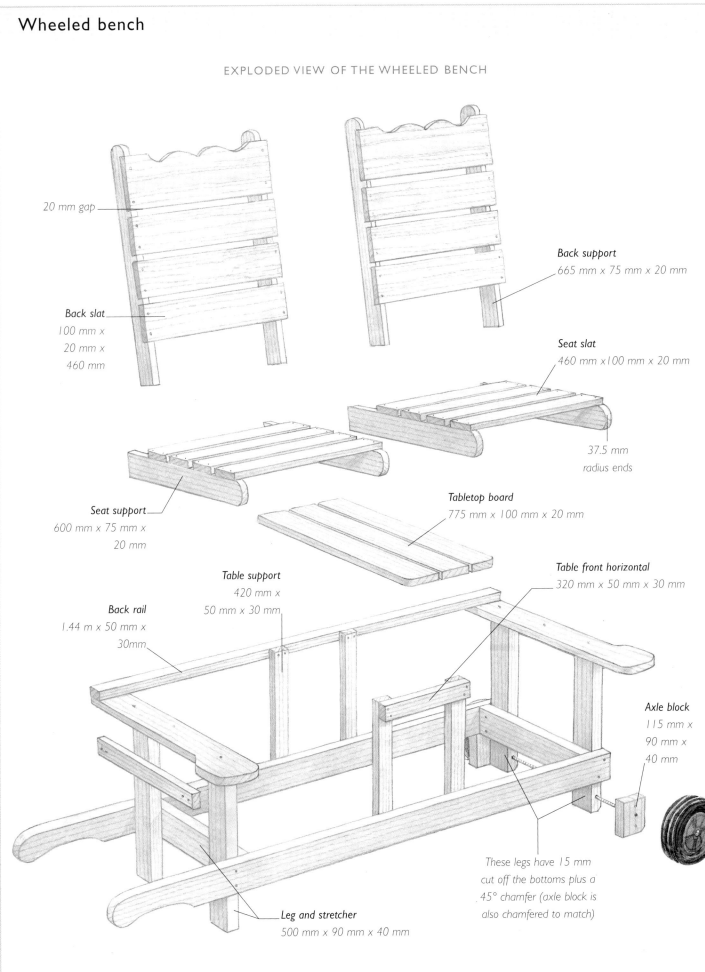

20 mm gap

Back support
665 mm x 75 mm x 20 mm

Back slat
100 mm x
20 mm x
460 mm

Seat slat
460 mm x100 mm x 20 mm

37.5 mm
radius ends

Seat support
600 mm x 75 mm x
20 mm

Tabletop board
775 mm x 100 mm x 20 mm

Table support
420 mm x
50 mm x 30 mm

Table front horizontal
320 mm x 50 mm x 30 mm

Back rail
1.44 m x 50 mm x
30mm

Axle block
115 mm x
90 mm x
40 mm

These legs have 15 mm
cut off the bottoms plus a
45° chamfer (axle block is
also chamfered to match)

Leg and stretcher
500 mm x 90 mm x 40 mm

FRONT VIEW OF THE WHEELED BENCH

Shaped backrest board
460 mm x 150 mm x 20 mm
1 grid square equals 20 mm

20 mm gap

Main handle
beam
1.8 m x
90 mm x
40 mm

Positioned 130 mm up from
the bottom of the legs

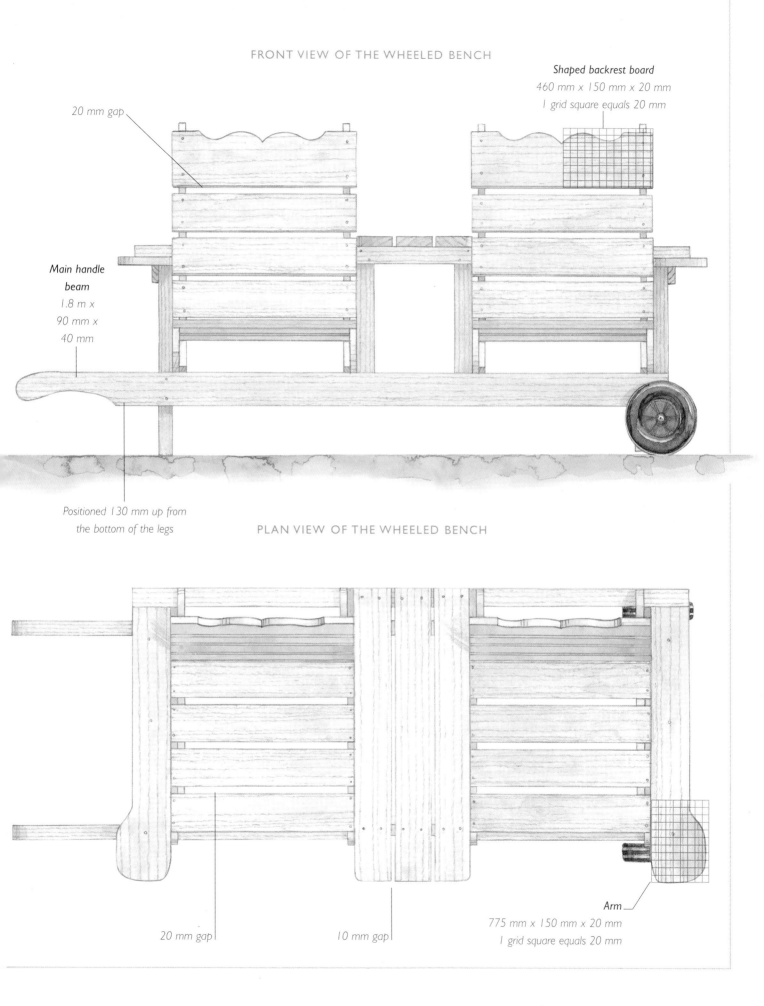

PLAN VIEW OF THE WHEELED BENCH

20 mm gap

10 mm gap

Arm

775 mm x 150 mm x 20 mm
1 grid square equals 20 mm

Step-by-step: **Making the wheeled bench**

Legs
Make sure that the legs are parallel to each other

Sawing the handle
Work slowly as the wood is very thick

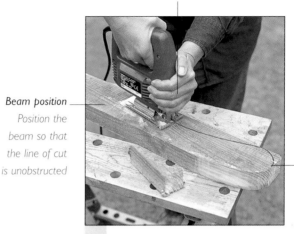

Sanding
Use the electric sander to soften the edges of the handle

Right angle
Check that the leg is square to the stretcher

Beam position
Position the beam so that the line of cut is unobstructed

1 With the crosscut saw, cut the legs and the stretchers to length (all at 500 mm), establish the position of the crossover, and fix with one 70 mm screw at each joint. Check for squareness and then drive in a second 70 mm screw.

2 Cut the handle beams to a length of 1.8 m with the crosscut saw. Next, draw the shape of the handle and fret out the profile with the jigsaw. Work in the direction of the end of the handle, to avoid cutting directly into end grain.

Tabletop position
Screw on one tabletop board to establish the middle of the table

Screw position
Make sure that the screws are centred in the thickness of the underarm support

Underarm support
Screw the support so that it is flush with the top of the legs

Marking
Use a square to mark in the position of the two flanking planks

Flush fit
Have the inside edge of the arm flush with the inside of the legs

3 Link the arms with the back support and screw it in place. Using 48 mm screws, screw on the table supports, fix the middle tabletop board to establish the centre of the table and then flank it with another tabletop board at each side.

4 Cut the arms to shape and sand them to a smooth finish. Using 48 mm screws, fix the underarm supports to the top of the legs (so the legs are set parallel) and then screw the arms in place with screws running into the supports.

Back support
Ease the bottom of the board
forward to make the back angle

End of cut
Run the cut to finish in
the central cleft

Clamping
Position and
clamp the
board so that
the cutting line
is unobstructed

Template
Use the waste
from cutting
the first half of
the design to
mark out the
other half

Screw position
Drive the
screws through
both boards
and into
the legs

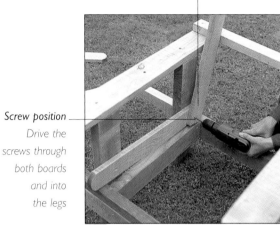

5 Take the two boards that go to make the seat supports, establish the correct canted angle, and fix them with 48 mm screws at the front end and the intersection of the two boards. Use a 70 mm screw (recessed in a 10 mm hole by 30 mm) from the back rail through into the edge of the back support.

6 Draw half of the cyma curve at the centre of the shaped backrest board and fret out with the jigsaw. Use the waste piece as a template to establish the other half of the design, and to create the total shape on the other shaped backrest board.

Back slats
Use waste pieces of
board as spacers

Threaded rod
Drill a hole for the rod (it
should not be a tight fit)

Fixing wheels
The order for
fixing the
wheels is
washer, nut,
washer, wheel,
washer, nut
and a final nut
to lock

Spacer
Use two
thicknesses of
waste board
to bring the
first board
up to the
correct height

Leg blocks
Chamfer the
corner of the
blocks and legs
with a saw

7 Screw the seat and back slats in place with 48 mm screws. Ensure that the spacing is correct by sliding pieces of waste wood between neighbouring boards.

8 Cut away the lower outside corners of the legs. Drill holes, 20 mm in diameter, through both the leg blocks and the legs, and then slide the axle in place. Finally, sand everything to a smooth finish, lay on a thin wash of paint and give the bench a coat of preservative.

Inspirations: Benches and chairs

Dreams about my childhood often feature an old oak bench in a neglected, overgrown orchard, dappled sunshine, buzzing insects and a rich carpet of fallen fruit! You may dedicate a lot of time to working on your garden to create a leafy heaven, but it is important to spend time actually sitting and enjoying the changing seasons and their cast of plants and flowers. A good selection of seats is vital.

RIGHT Swinging benches are a great place to while away an afternoon. Incorporating one into an arbour makes a delightful feature, which is very pleasant to sit in when surrounded by scented climbers.

ABOVE A grand bench and a modern push-along lounger provide a variety of seating options on this patio, to suit both mood and weather.

LEFT A well-worn rocker nestles in a glade of rough grass, surrounded by foraging hens. Its weathered appearance suits the informal backdrop perfectly.

Romantic arch

This project really comes into its own in summer – there is something gloriously exciting about a wooden arch heavy with clematis and honeysuckle, and it makes a really beautiful feature. Position it at the entrance point to a garden area, where it will frame the vista behind it, or site it midway along a path to add a romantic touch.

TIME

A full weekend (about twelve hours for the woodwork, and four hours for putting together and finishing).

USEFUL TIP

Avoid using a wood treatment such as creosote, because it will cause some plants to shrivel on contact. Use a water-based finish – for example matt white paint.

YOU WILL NEED

Materials *for an arch 1.150 m wide, 440 mm deep and 2.250 m high. (All rough-sawn pine pieces include excess length for wastage.)*
• Pine: 4 pieces, each 2 m long, 75 mm square (posts)
• Pine: 20 pieces, each 2 m long, 50 mm wide and 30 mm thick (cross ties)
• Pine: 1 piece, 1 m long, 75 mm x 75 mm triangular section (capital cross ties)
• Pine: 4 pieces, each 2 m long, 150 mm wide and 20 mm thick (arch laminations)
• Galvanized and painted spiked post supports: 4 (one for each post)
• Zinc-plated, countersunk screws:
100 x 38 mm no. 8,
100 x 65 mm no. 10
• Exterior-quality matt white paint

Tools
• Pencil, ruler, tape measure, compass, engineer's protractor, bevel gauge and square
• Two portable workbenches
• Plywood workboard, about 1 m square
• Electric jigsaw
• Large clamp
• Cordless electric drill with a cross-point screwdriver bit
• Drill bits to match the screw sizes
• Electric sander with a pack of medium-grade sandpaper
• Crosscut saw
• Mallet
• Bevel-edged chisel: 50 mm
• Sledgehammer
• Spanner to fit the post support nuts
• Paintbrush: 40 mm

UNDERNEATH THE ARCHES

The clever thing about this structure is the way that the arch tops consist of a number of identical components. Each is made up of eight curvy-shaped boards (one cut in half), which are cut from 150 mm-wide board and laminated together with screws. Once made, the arches are screwed into the half-laps at the top of the posts, and the whole thing is held together and braced with cross ties. We used ties 50 mm wide and 30 mm thick for running up the sides of the posts and over the arch, and two triangular-section ties to act as capitals at the point where the arched top joints into the posts. Finally, just to make sure that the structure stays put, the four posts are located in spiked post supports. The finished arch is an ideal structure for hanging a gate – see the Picket Gate project on page 46.

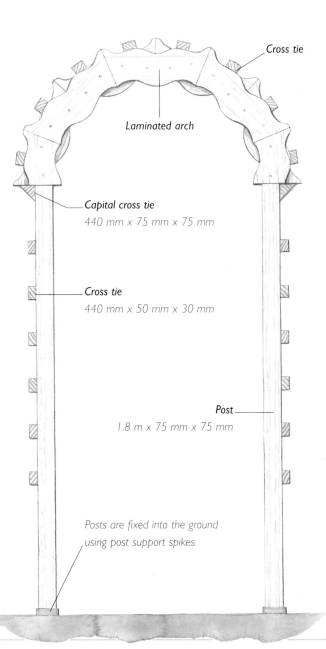

FRONT VIEW OF THE ROMANTIC ARCH

Cross tie

Laminated arch

Capital cross tie
440 mm x 75 mm x 75 mm

Cross tie
440 mm x 50 mm x 30 mm

Post
1.8 m x 75 mm x 75 mm

Posts are fixed into the ground using post support spikes

Romantic arch

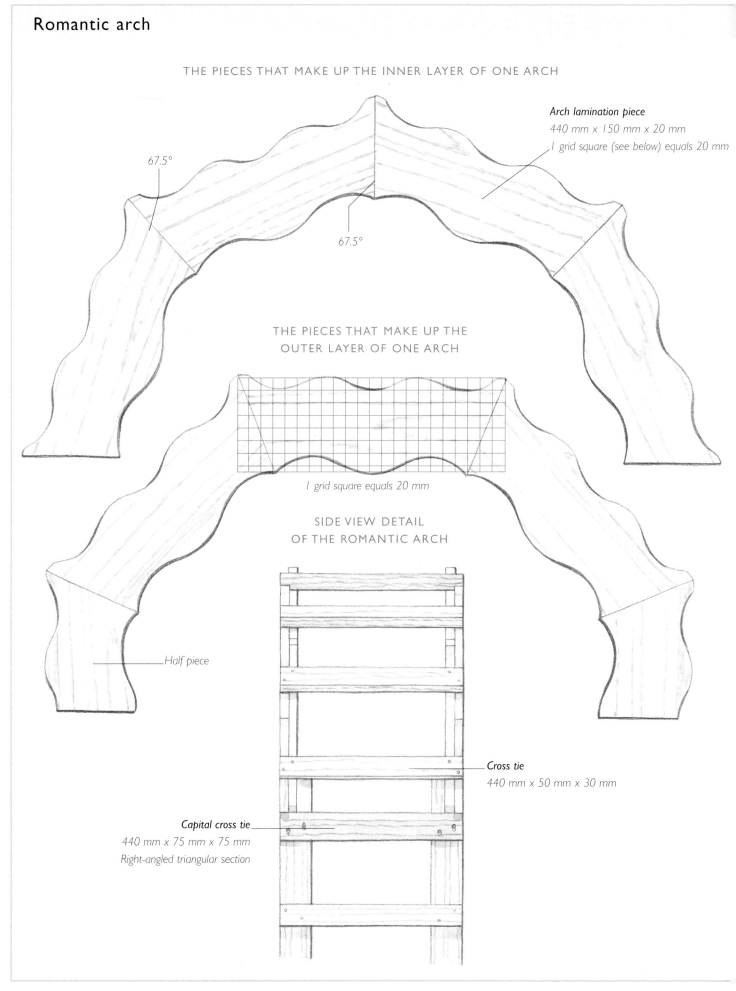

THE PIECES THAT MAKE UP THE INNER LAYER OF ONE ARCH

Arch lamination piece
440 mm x 150 mm x 20 mm
1 grid square (see below) equals 20 mm

67.5°

67.5°

THE PIECES THAT MAKE UP THE
OUTER LAYER OF ONE ARCH

1 grid square equals 20 mm

SIDE VIEW DETAIL
OF THE ROMANTIC ARCH

Half piece

Cross tie
440 mm x 50 mm x 30 mm

Capital cross tie
440 mm x 75 mm x 75 mm
Right-angled triangular section

EXPLODED VIEW OF THE ROMANTIC ARCH

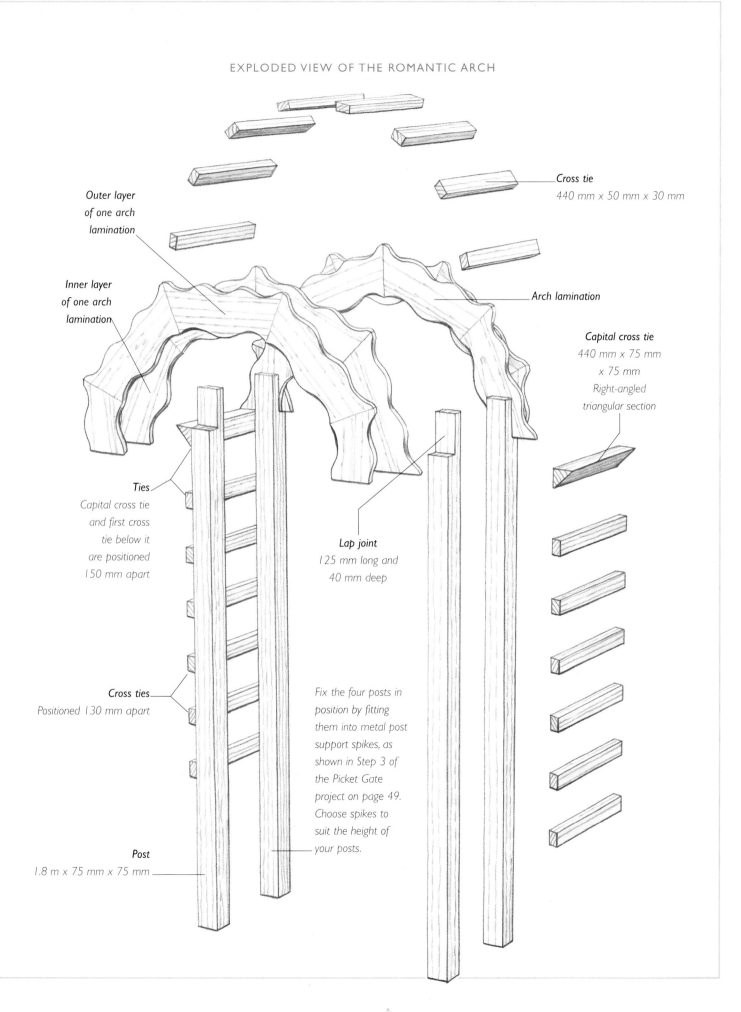

Cross tie
440 mm x 50 mm x 30 mm

Outer layer
of one arch
lamination

Inner layer
of one arch
lamination

Arch lamination

Capital cross tie
*440 mm x 75 mm
x 75 mm
Right-angled
triangular section*

Ties
*Capital cross tie
and first cross
tie below it
are positioned
150 mm apart*

Lap joint
*125 mm long and
40 mm deep*

Cross ties
Positioned 130 mm apart

*Fix the four posts in
position by fitting
them into metal post
support spikes, as
shown in Step 3 of
the Picket Gate
project on page 49.
Choose spikes to
suit the height of
your posts.*

Post
1.8 m x 75 mm x 75 mm

Step-by-step: **Making the romantic arch**

Sawing square
Hold the saw at right
angles to the wood

Template
Use the piece of waste
as a template

Cutting angle
Neighbouring
boards share
the same
67.5° cut

Holding firm
If you can't
hold the wood
with your hand,
use a clamp to
hold it down

1 Fix the engineer's protractor to an angle of 67.5° and set out the sixteen boards that make up the arch laminations for the top of the arch. The longest side of each board should measure 440 mm from point to point.

2 Draw the curved profile of the arch lamination on one board and use the jigsaw to fret it out. Use the waste pieces as templates to help you draw the shapes on the other fifteen boards.

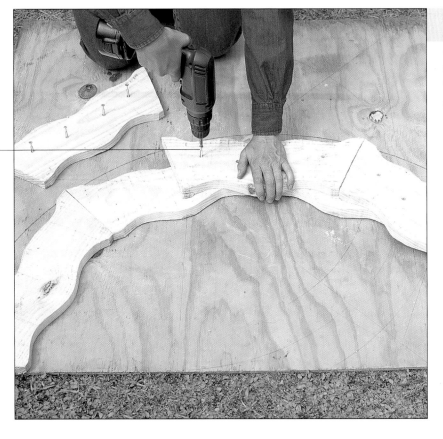

3 Sandwich and clamp the boards together to make the double-thickness shape and fix together with 38 mm screws. You will need two half-boards to complete each form.

Screwing
Run four
screws in from
one side

Helpful hint

When you have lots of pieces to fit together, as in this design, you may find that inaccuracies in marking out and cutting are amplified. To avoid problems, arrange the pieces that make up the arch (without screwing them), check they fit well and make adjustments as necessary.

Lapped ends
*The end of the arch fits squarely
against the top of the post*

4 Set out the top of the posts with laps at 125 mm long and 40 mm deep, and cut them out with the crosscut saw, mallet and chisel. Screw the arch in place in the lap with 65 mm screws. Repeat this sequence for the other arch.

Waste block
Use the lap waste to lift the arch up to the correct height

Flush fit
The face of the arch must be flush with the face of the post

Angled screws
Run the screws in at a slight angle

Tie position
Centre the cross ties between humps

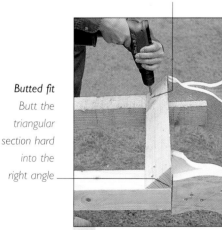

Butted fit
Butt the triangular section hard into the right angle

Screwholes
Drill holes for the screws

Parallel ties
Ensure that the cross ties are parallel to each other

5 Cut the triangular section for the capital cross ties into two lengths of 440 mm and use 65 mm screws to fix them in place so that they are butted hard up against the underside edge of the bottom of the laminated arch.

6 Using 38 mm screws, fix all the cross ties up the posts and over the arch. Rub down the arch to remove splinters, give it a generous coat of white paint, and fix in the spiked supports as shown in the Picket Gate project (see page 46).

Corner patio planter

If your patio is dotted with a colourful collection of little pot plants, which are forever

being knocked over by children or pets, this is the perfect project for you. Gather up

your plants, arrange them in the planter, and you have an enviable patio feature that

keeps the area tidy and displays the plants attractively.

TIME

A weekend (twelve hours for the woodwork and a few hours for finishing).

USEFUL TIP

The joints are slightly tricky to cut, so take your time.

YOU WILL NEED

Materials *for a planter 565 mm high and 950 mm square. (All rough-sawn pine pieces include excess length for wastage.)*

- Pine: 1 piece, 2 m long and 75 mm square (main posts)
- Pine: 7 pieces, each 2 m long, 100 mm wide and 25 mm thick (back and front pickets)
- Pine: 4 pieces, each 2 m long, 150 mm wide and 20 mm thick (front rails, floorboards, post capitals)
- Pine: 2 pieces, each 2 m long, 50 mm wide and 35 mm thick (back rails)
- Zinc-plated, countersunk cross-headed screws: 100 x 38 mm no. 8
- Acrylic paint in colour to suit
- Clear preservative

Tools

- Pencil, ruler, tape measure, compass, bevel gauge and square
- Portable workbench
- Flexible metal metre rule
- Electric jigsaw
- Crosscut saw
- Tenon saw
- Cordless electric drill and cross-point screwdriver bit
- Drill bit, 20 mm wide (for boring out the mortises)
- Mallet
- Bevel-edged chisel, 35 mm wide
- Drill bits to match screws
- Electric sander with a pack of medium-grade sandpaper
- Paintbrush: 30 mm wide

COMPLETELY CORNERED

The design brief for this project was six-fold. The planter had to be raised up off the ground, it had to fit into a right-angled corner, it had to present a curved front, it had to look good alongside a picket fence, it had be scaled and detailed so it suited a cottage garden, and it had to be strong.

In many ways, the resulting design is very straightforward — really it is just a right-angled box with pickets to the sides. However, the curved front rails and the mortise and tenon joints make it a little more complex. The front rails are slightly unusual in that the tenons run at a skewed angle into the mortises. The joints aren't particularly difficult to cut, but you do need to spend longer than usual at the setting out stage. When we came to painting the finished piece, we decided that the only way to achieve a subtle colour was to water down the acrylic paint to a thin wash, and then to top this with a coat of clear preservative.

FRONT VIEW OF THE
CORNER PATIO PLANTER

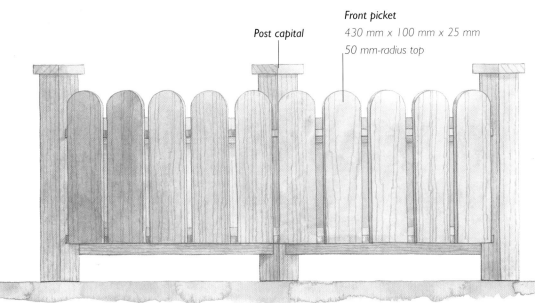

Post capital

Front picket
430 mm x 100 mm x 25 mm
50 mm-radius top

Corner patio planter

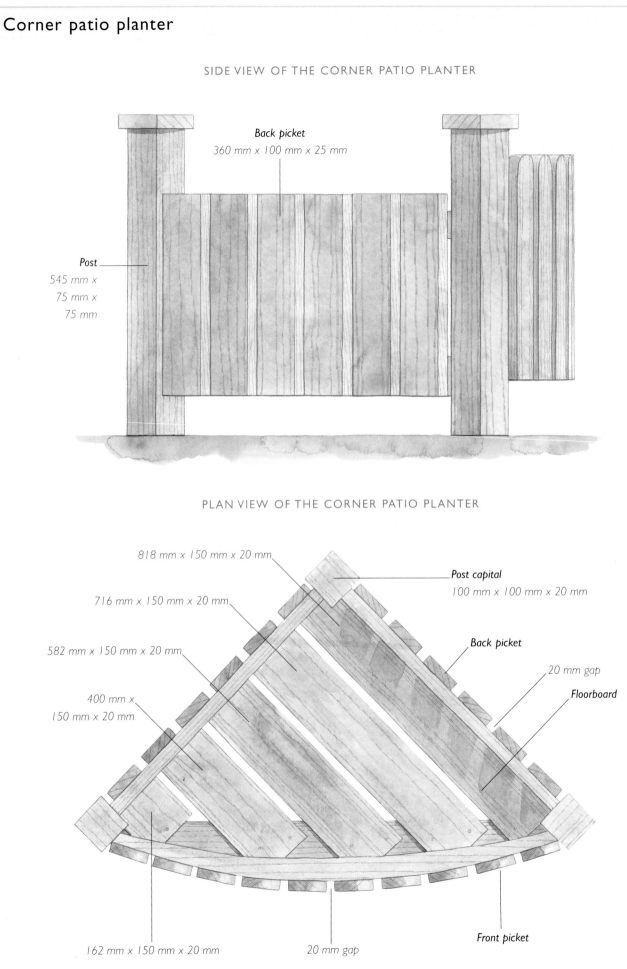

SIDE VIEW OF THE CORNER PATIO PLANTER

Back picket
360 mm x 100 mm x 25 mm

Post
545 mm x
75 mm x
75 mm

PLAN VIEW OF THE CORNER PATIO PLANTER

818 mm x 150 mm x 20 mm

Post capital
100 mm x 100 mm x 20 mm

716 mm x 150 mm x 20 mm

Back picket

582 mm x 150 mm x 20 mm

20 mm gap

Floorboard

400 mm x
150 mm x 20 mm

162 mm x 150 mm x 20 mm

20 mm gap

Front picket

EXPLODED VIEW OF THE CORNER PATIO PLANTER

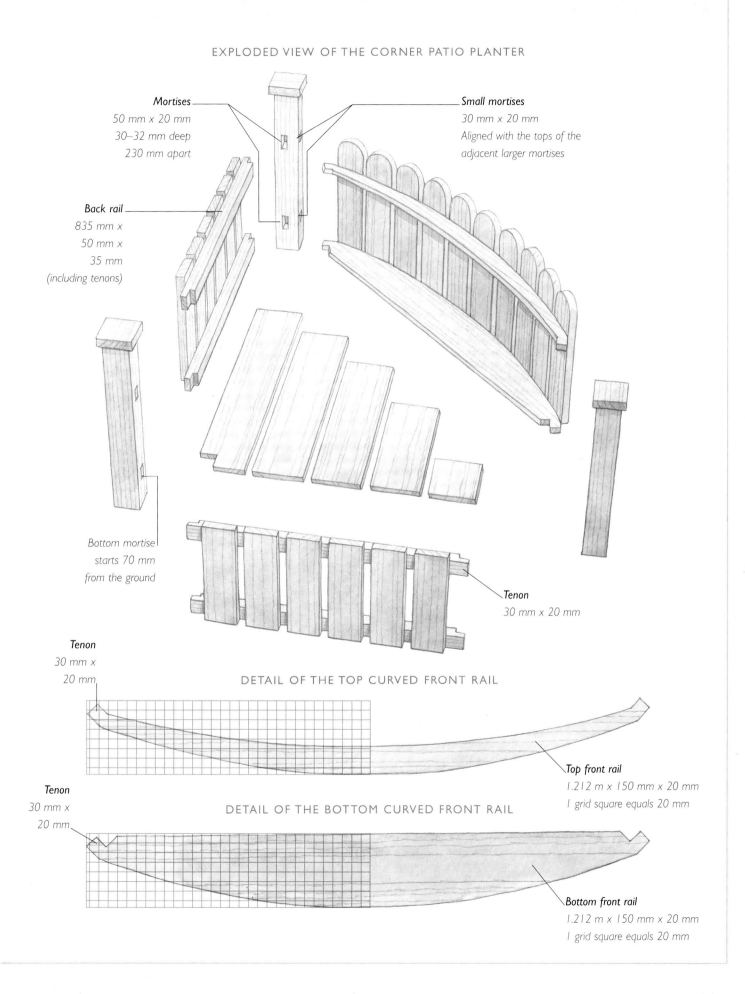

Mortises
50 mm x 20 mm
30–32 mm deep
230 mm apart

Small mortises
30 mm x 20 mm
Aligned with the tops of the
adjacent larger mortises

Back rail
835 mm x
50 mm x
35 mm
(including tenons)

*Bottom mortise
starts 70 mm
from the ground*

Tenon
30 mm x 20 mm

Tenon
30 mm x
20 mm

DETAIL OF THE TOP CURVED FRONT RAIL

Top front rail
1.212 m x 150 mm x 20 mm
I grid square equals 20 mm

Tenon
30 mm x
20 mm

DETAIL OF THE BOTTOM CURVED FRONT RAIL

Bottom front rail
1.212 m x 150 mm x 20 mm
I grid square equals 20 mm

Step-by-step: Making the corner patio planter

Marking the curve
*Bend the rule to mark out one
half of the curve at a time*

Cutting the tenon
*Cut down the grain of the wood
to the waste side of the line*

Nails
*Secure the
end of the
rule between
two nails*

Sawing
*Use your
forefinger to
help set the
angle of the
saw cut*

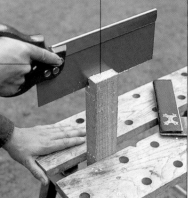

1 Set out the design of the curved front rails on the 150 mm-wide board. Use the metal rule to achieve the shape of the curve. Fret out the profile with the jigsaw.

2 Set out the ends of the straight back rails with tenons 30 mm long and 20 mm wide, the waste piece measuring 30 mm long and 15 mm wide. Cut the joint with the crosscut and tenon saws and tidy up with the chisel.

Chisel
*Square the back of the
chisel with the line*

Securing
*Make sure that
the post is
tightly clamped
in the bench*

Screwing
*Run a screw
through the
mortise and
tenon joint*

Bottom board
*The wide
board goes at
the bottom*

3 Cut the three main posts to length and set out the position of the mortises. Clear the bulk of the mortise waste with the drill and then cut back to the line with the mallet and chisel.

4 Assemble the frame, knock the joints home and clench them with screws. The bottom board is positioned so that the generous straight edge becomes a support for the floorboards.

Notched board
Cut the first board so that
it fits around the post

5 Cut the waste lengths of board to make floorboards that fit inside the base, spacing them about 20 mm apart, and fix with screws. The floorboards can be left square-cut where they fit the front rail, but the longest board needs to be notched to fit around the back post.

Helpful hint

If you have plenty of wood to spare and you want to make the finish of the base neater, the ends of the floorboards can be cut to fit the shape of the curved front rail piece.

Board ends
Save time
by leaving
the board
ends square

6 Cut semicircular radius curves on top of the front pickets. Screw the pickets in place, so that they are spaced by the thickness of a board, and so that the bottom edge of the picket is flush with the underside of the front rail. Cut three post capitals (100 mm square and 20 mm thick) and screw them in place on top of the posts. Finally, sand the planter, then paint it and coat with preservative.

Bottom of
picket
The bottom of
the pickets
should be flush
with the rail

Spacer
Use a piece of
scrap wood for
a spacer

Potting table

A potting table is a real boon to keen gardeners. No more stooping to dip into massive bags of compost, or fumbling around looking for a level surface to work on. You simply fill the table's side tray with compost, line up flowerpots and plants, and get on with potting. Everything you need is comfortably to hand.

YOU WILL NEED

Materials *for a potting table 1.295 m wide, 662 mm deep and 1.574 m high. (All rough-sawn pine pieces include excess length for wastage.)*
- Pine: 3 pieces, each 3 m long, 90 mm wide, 40 mm thick (front and back legs)
- Pine: 3 pieces, each 3 m long, 100 mm wide, 20 mm thick (end boards, top and bottom horizontal rails, tray pieces, peg board)
- Pine: 1 piece, 1 m long, 30 mm wide, 20 mm thick (tray corner support blocks)
- Pine: 3 pieces, each 3 m long, 150 mm wide and 22 mm thick (tray base, table base, tabletop, decorative back board, brackets, top shelf)

- Dowel: 1 piece, 1 m long and 22 mm in diameter (pegs)
- Waterproof glue
- Zinc-plated, countersunk cross-headed screws: 100 x 38 mm no. 8
- Teak oil

Tools
- Pencil, ruler, tracing paper and square
- Portable workbench
- Crosscut saw
- Cordless electric drill with a cross-point screwdriver bit
- Selection of drill bits
- Electric jigsaw
- Electric sander with a pack of medium-grade sandpaper
- Paintbrush: 40 mm

SIDE VIEW OF THE POTTING TABLE

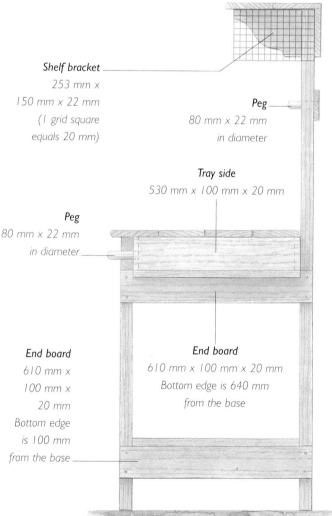

Shelf bracket
253 mm x
150 mm x 22 mm
(1 grid square equals 20 mm)

Peg
80 mm x 22 mm in diameter

Tray side
530 mm x 100 mm x 20 mm

Peg
80 mm x 22 mm in diameter

End board
610 mm x 100 mm x 20 mm
Bottom edge is 100 mm from the base

End board
610 mm x 100 mm x 20 mm
Bottom edge is 640 mm from the base

A POTTING TABLE FOR ALL SEASONS

The total height of the bench is 1.574 m, with the worksurface set at 862 mm high. The top horizontal rails, which link the legs and support the worksurface at back and front, also run through to the right-hand side of the worksurface to form the sides of the compost tray. If you are left-handed, all you do is modify the design so that the rails run through to the other end of the bench. The structure is simple and direct – there are no complicated joints to cut and the horizontal members are butted and screwed to the vertical posts. In use, the tray is filled with compost, small tools are hung on the pegs, seed packets and other items are stored on the top shelf, and of course the base surface is just right for stacking flowerpots and a watering can. Note how the work-surface boards are butted edge to edge, while the base surface boards are spaced to allow for easy cleaning.

It's a perfect no-nonsense piece of garden furniture, which draws inspiration from early nineteenth-century furniture designs in featuring smooth cyma curves on the back board and the brackets. If you are a keen gardener and enjoy taking cuttings and potting on plants, this potting table will contribute something special to your workshop or greenhouse.

Potting table

FRONT VIEW OF THE POTTING TABLE

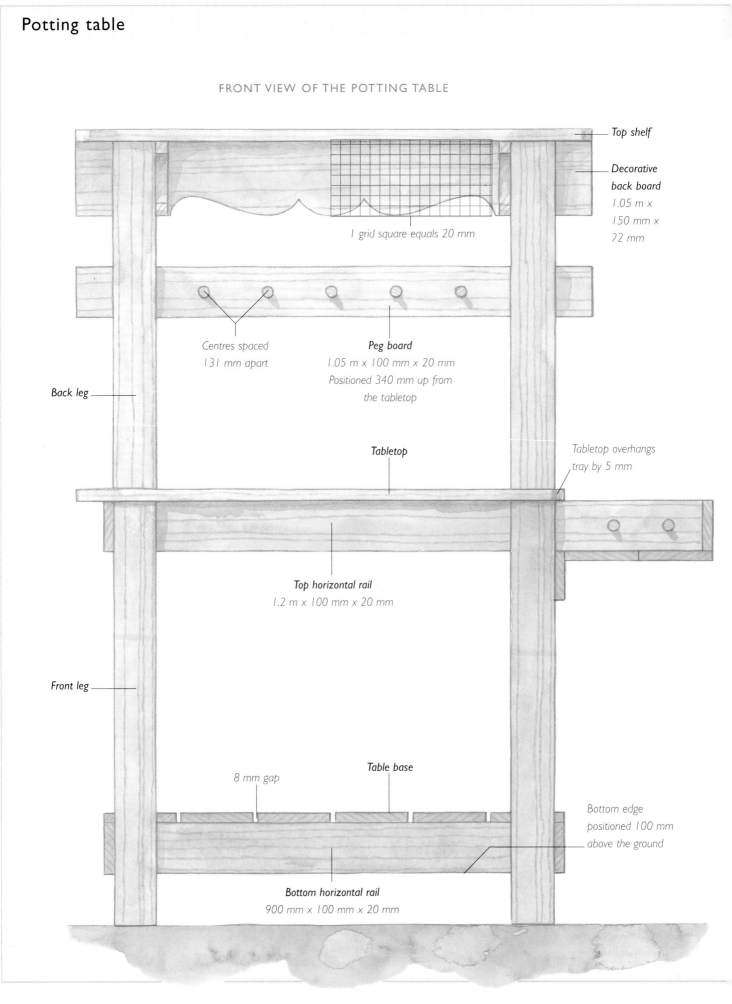

Top shelf

Decorative
back board
1.05 m x
150 mm x
22 mm

1 grid square equals 20 mm

Centres spaced
131 mm apart

Peg board
1.05 m x 100 mm x 20 mm
Positioned 340 mm up from
the tabletop

Back leg

Tabletop

Tabletop overhangs
tray by 5 mm

Top horizontal rail
1.2 m x 100 mm x 20 mm

Front leg

Table base

8 mm gap

Bottom edge
positioned 100 mm
above the ground

Bottom horizontal rail
900 mm x 100 mm x 20 mm

EXPLODED VIEW OF THE POTTING TABLE

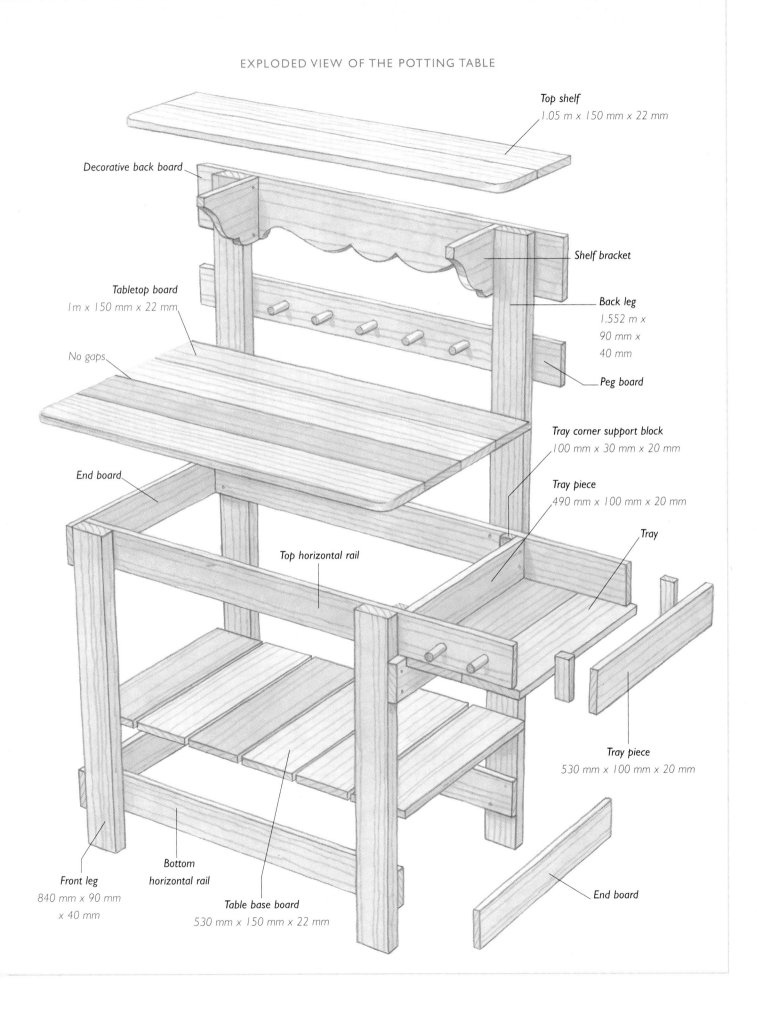

Top shelf
1.05 m x 150 mm x 22 mm

Decorative back board

Shelf bracket

Tabletop board
1m x 150 mm x 22 mm

Back leg
*1.552 m x
90 mm x
40 mm*

No gaps

Peg board

Tray corner support block
100 mm x 30 mm x 20 mm

End board

Tray piece
490 mm x 100 mm x 20 mm

Tray

Top horizontal rail

Front leg
*840 mm x 90 mm
x 40 mm*

Bottom
horizontal rail

Table base board
530 mm x 150 mm x 22 mm

Tray piece
530 mm x 100 mm x 20 mm

End board

Step-by-step: **Making the potting table**

Square
The horizontal rails must be square to the legs

Tray corner support block
Screw blocks to hold the tray sides in place

Parallel
Make sure that the two legs are parallel to each other

Leg position
The leg is on the outside of the frame

Tight fit
Push the end board hard under the top horizontal rail

1 Use the crosscut saw to cut all the wood to size. Set out the two 1.552 m-long back legs, linking them with the top and bottom horizontal boards, check for squareness, and then run pilot holes through the boards and fix them with two screws at each intersection.

2 Having built both the front and back units, complete with pegholes in the tray end of the top horizontal rail, link them together with the four 610 mm-long end boards. Screw on the corner support blocks for fitting the two tray pieces.

3 Set the four 1 m-long, 150 mm-wide tabletop boards in position so that they are butted hard up against the two back posts. Leave a 5 mm overhang on the right-hand side, so that the surface hangs over the tray. Check for squareness and fix with screws.

Board position
Push the board hard up against the back posts

Helpful hint

Before you fix the tabletop boards in place, check that the potting table is square. Use a large square or a tape measure to check that the diagonal measurements are identical.

Shelf bracket
Fit the board at right
angles to the back post

4 Trace off the cyma curves
of the decorative back
board and shelf brackets, transfer
the lines through to the wood,
and cut the curves with the
jigsaw. Screw the back board and
brackets in place so that their
top edges are flush with the top
of the back posts. Drill and fit
the peg board.

Screwing
Run two
screws through
the bracket
and into the
back post

Cyma curve
Sand the
curve to a
smooth finish

Screwing
Fix the planks with two
screws at each end

Sandpaper
Make a double fold
of sandpaper

Sanding
Rub the end of
the peg to a
rounded finish

Screwholes
Drill a hole for
each screw
that is near the
end of a plank

5 Fix all the other members in place
(the boards for the base of the table,
and the boards on the underside and ends
of the tray). Position the table base boards
flush with the horizontal rails that link the
legs, but spaced by 8 mm.

6 Use the graded sandpapers to round
over the ends of the pegs, and to
generally bring all the edges and corners to
a slightly rounded finish. Finally, give all the
surfaces a coat of teak oil.

Rabbit ark

Children love rabbits, so why not give them a couple of furry friends to play with? The new members of the family will need housing, and that's where our ark comes in. It folds up for easy transport and has handles so that you can move it around the garden (position it in different locations for the rabbits to trim your lawn).

EXPLODED VIEW OF THE RABBIT ARK

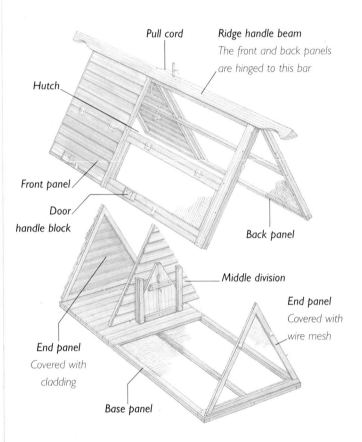

Pull cord

Ridge handle beam
The front and back panels are hinged to this bar

Hutch

Front panel

Door

handle block

End panel
Covered with cladding

Base panel

Middle division

End panel
Covered with wire mesh

Back panel

A-FRAME RABBIT HOME

The clever thing about this rabbit ark is the fact that it folds up for transport and storage. While in essence the ark is made up from seven component parts (a base, two long sides, three triangular divisions and a carrying beam), the ingenious design means that it can be swiftly broken down into three flat-pack units. These are the two sides, which hinge to the handle beam like a book; the base, complete with the two hinged ends; and the middle division.

To put the ark together, set the base flat on the grass, open up the two triangular ends, locate the middle division on its dowels, open the book-like sides and drop them over the ends, and then do up all the latches. When you want to move the ark, ask a friend to help and simply lift it up by the beam handles. To shut the rabbits in for the night, wait until they are safely in the enclosed hutch end, unhitch the pull cord and lower the portcullis door.

YOU WILL NEED

Materials *for a rabbit ark 2.405 m long, 769 mm high and 830 mm wide. (All rough-sawn pine pieces include excess length for wastage.)*
- Pine: 15 pieces, each 3 m long, 35 mm wide and 20 mm thick (for all the frames and corner trim)
- Pine: 4 pieces, each 3 m long, 75 mm wide and 20 mm thick (floorboards)
- Pine: 1 piece, 3 m long, 75 mm triangular section, 100 mm across the hypotenuse (ridge handle beam)
- Pine: 1 piece, 1 m long, 50 mm wide and 34 mm thick (door handle blocks)
- Pine: 1 piece, 2 m long, 75 mm wide and 20 mm thick (end frame trim)
- Pine feather-edged board: 20 pieces, each 3 m long, 100 mm wide and 10 mm thick (for cladding the walls of the hutch end of the ark)
- Pine: 1 piece, 1 m long, 150 mm wide and 22 mm thick (portcullis door)
- Pine dowel: 2 pieces, 300 mm long, one 6 mm in diameter and the other 12 mm (for locating the middle division and making the pull cord)
- Galvanized rabbit wire: 6 m roll, 1 m wide (cage)

- Galvanized staples: 1 kg x 10 mm
- Galvanized butt door hinges: 14 x 60 mm long, 20 mm wide, with screws to fit
- Plated snap-fit case latches: 8 medium size, with screws
- Zinc-plated, countersunk cross-headed screws: 100 x 20 mm no. 8, 100 x 38 mm no. 8, 10 x 50 mm no. 10, 100 x 65 mm no. 10
- Exterior-quality PVA glue
- Nylon cord (for door pull)
- Clear preservative

Tools
- Pencil, ruler, tape measure, marking gauge and square
- Two portable workbenches
- Crosscut saw
- Cordless electric drill with a cross-point screwdriver bit
- Drill bits to match the screw sizes
- Wire snips
- Small hammer
- Electric jigsaw
- Drill bit to match the dowel size
- Electric sander with a pack of medium-grade sandpaper
- Small screwdriver to fit the hinge and latch screws
- Paintbrush: 40 mm

Rabbit ark

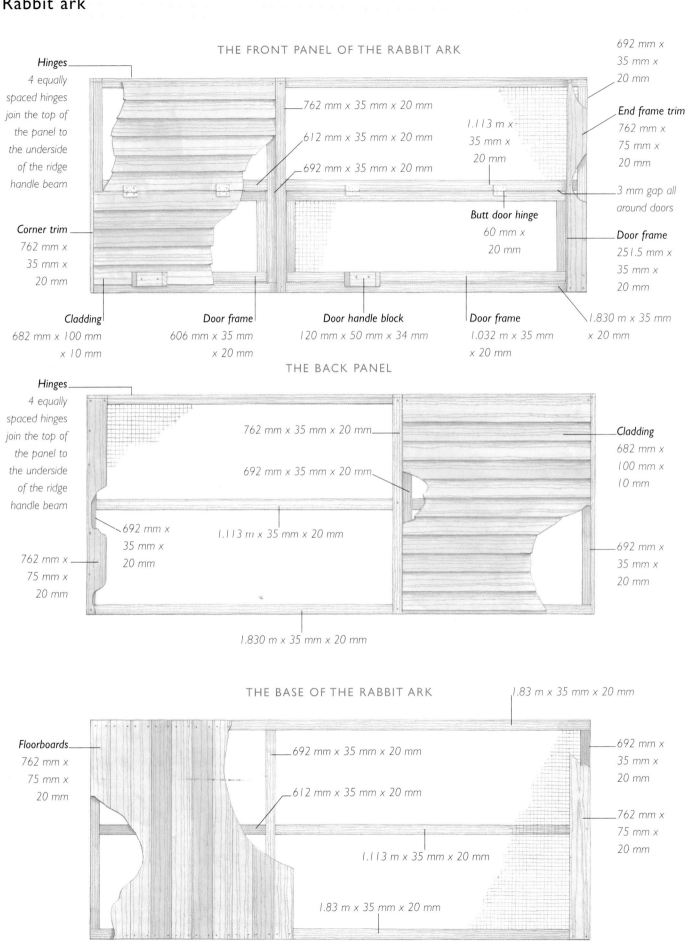

THE FRONT PANEL OF THE RABBIT ARK

Hinges
4 equally spaced hinges join the top of the panel to the underside of the ridge handle beam

762 mm x 35 mm x 20 mm

612 mm x 35 mm x 20 mm

692 mm x 35 mm x 20 mm

692 mm x 35 mm x 20 mm

End frame trim
762 mm x 75 mm x 20 mm

1.113 m x 35 mm x 20 mm

3 mm gap all around doors

Butt door hinge
60 mm x 20 mm

Corner trim
762 mm x 35 mm x 20 mm

Door frame
251.5 mm x 35 mm x 20 mm

Cladding
682 mm x 100 mm x 10 mm

Door frame
606 mm x 35 mm x 20 mm

Door handle block
120 mm x 50 mm x 34 mm

Door frame
1.032 m x 35 mm x 20 mm

1.830 m x 35 mm x 20 mm

THE BACK PANEL

Hinges
4 equally spaced hinges join the top of the panel to the underside of the ridge handle beam

762 mm x 35 mm x 20 mm

692 mm x 35 mm x 20 mm

692 mm x 35 mm x 20 mm

1.113 m x 35 mm x 20 mm

Cladding
682 mm x 100 mm x 10 mm

762 mm x 75 mm x 20 mm

692 mm x 35 mm x 20 mm

1.830 m x 35 mm x 20 mm

THE BASE OF THE RABBIT ARK

1.83 m x 35 mm x 20 mm

Floorboards
762 mm x 75 mm x 20 mm

692 mm x 35 mm x 20 mm

612 mm x 35 mm x 20 mm

692 mm x 35 mm x 20 mm

762 mm x 75 mm x 20 mm

1.113 m x 35 mm x 20 mm

1.83 m x 35 mm x 20 mm

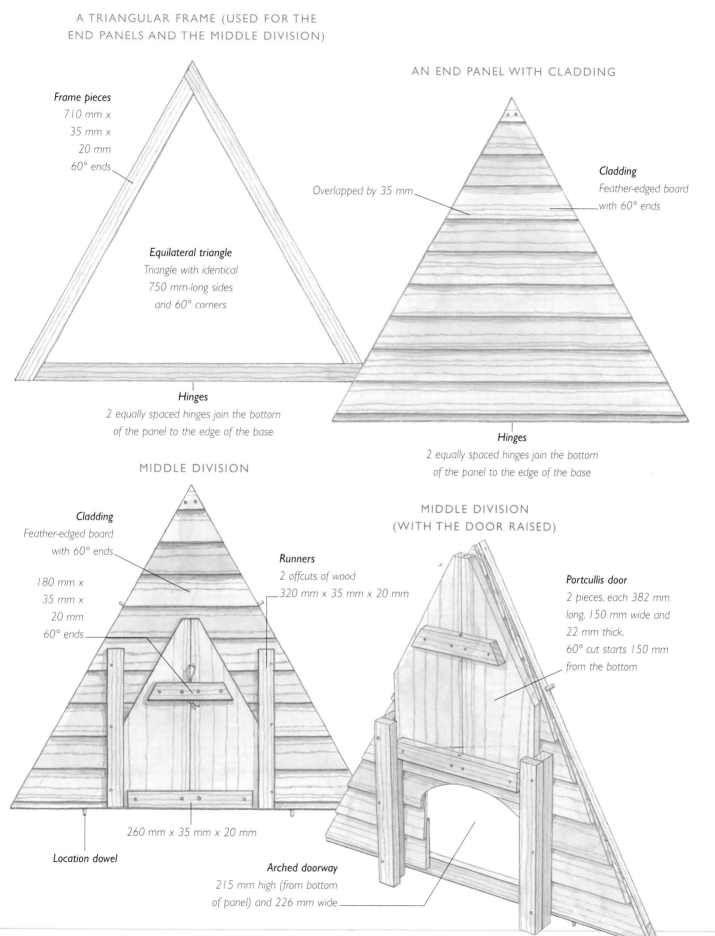

A TRIANGULAR FRAME (USED FOR THE
END PANELS AND THE MIDDLE DIVISION)

Frame pieces
710 mm x
35 mm x
20 mm
60° ends

Equilateral triangle
Triangle with identical
750 mm-long sides
and 60° corners

Hinges
2 equally spaced hinges join the bottom
of the panel to the edge of the base

AN END PANEL WITH CLADDING

Cladding
Feather-edged board
with 60° ends

Overlapped by 35 mm

Hinges
2 equally spaced hinges join the bottom
of the panel to the edge of the base

MIDDLE DIVISION

Cladding
Feather-edged board
with 60° ends

180 mm x
35 mm x
20 mm
60° ends

Runners
2 offcuts of wood
320 mm x 35 mm x 20 mm

260 mm x 35 mm x 20 mm

Location dowel

Arched doorway
215 mm high (from bottom
of panel) and 226 mm wide

MIDDLE DIVISION
(WITH THE DOOR RAISED)

Portcullis door
2 pieces, each 382 mm
long, 150 mm wide and
22 mm thick.
60° cut starts 150 mm
from the bottom

Step-by-step: **Making the rabbit ark**

Screwing
Fix each joint
with two screws

Support boards
Clamp boards
in the
workbench to
support the
frame

1 Cut the lengths of wood that make up the frame, butt joint them together and fix with 65 mm screws. Build all eight frames: the base, the front panel, the back panel, the two doors in the front panel, and the three triangles that make up the end panels and middle division. Screw the door handle blocks in place on the doors with 50 mm screws.

Rabbit wire
Cut the wire about 10 mm
smaller than the frame all around

Cutting
It may help to
bend the wire
out of the way
of the snips as
you cut

Supports
Rest the frame
on a couple of
spare boards

2 Set the base down flat on a couple of spare pieces of wood, and use the wire snips to cut the rabbit wire to fit. Cut the large pieces first. Hammer in staples at about 50 mm intervals. Screw the corner trim in place on the front panel using 38 mm screws (see working drawing).

Screwholes
Drill holes through the feather-edged
board to take the screws

Jig
Use a simple
jig to help you
space the
boards equally

3 Clad the frames with feather-edged board. When you are doing this, use a little scrap of wood, marked off at 65 mm, to ensure that the board overlap is always constant at about 35 mm. Screw the boards in place with 20 mm screws.

Cord loop
Tie a loop for attaching
the pull cord

Door runners
The door
should be a
loose fit within
the runners

Bevel
Saw a bevel on
the underside
of the top of
the door

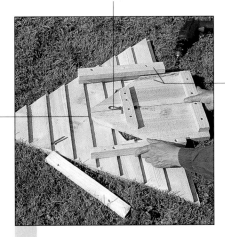

4 Cut out the door hole in the middle division with the jigsaw and build the two door-slide runners from lengths of 35 mm-wide, 20 mm-thick offcuts. Make the door from two lengths of 150 mm-wide board and trim it to fit.

Door pull cord
The door pull cord, complete with the 12 mm dowel handle, runs down through a hole
in the ridge handle beam to link up with a looped cord on the top of the sliding door

Location
dowels
Spread glue
inside the hole
and then tap
the dowel
in place

Alignment
Double-check
that the dowels
locate in the
holes in the
floor panel

5 Drill and glue-fit two lengths of 6 mm dowel into the underside edge of the middle division. Set the partition upright on the floor to establish its position, and drill matching location holes in the floor beam.

Helpful hint

If you make a mistake while positioning the location holes for the dowels, leave the location dowel where it is, and plug the location hole with a piece of dowel. Wait for the glue to dry, then sand the plugged dowel flush. Drill another hole.

Fixing hinges
Screw the hinges to the frame
first and then to the handle beam

Alignment
Before you fit the latches, ensure the
end panel is flush with the sides

Prop the sides
Ask a friend
to hold the
side panels at
the angle
shown here

Latches
Have a trial
run for fitting a
latch so that
you know how
far apart the
two pieces
should be

Screwing
Drill pilot holes
for the screws
and use the
correct size of
screwdriver

6 Saw and sand the ends of the triangular-section ridge handle beam to make comfortable handles, and screw hinges in place, centring the two sides on the beam's 100 mm hypotenuse.

7 Use 38 mm screws to fit the two 75 mm-wide pieces of end frame trim, to strengthen the end of the cage, and then screw the snap-fit latches in place at a point about two-thirds of the way up the sides of the triangle. Thread and fit the door-pull cord. Paint with preservative.

Classic pergola

If you want to create an instant feature in your garden, which establishes a focal point and invites visitors to wander under it, consider the merits of a pergola. It provides a place to sit in the shade, a spot for children to play, somewhere to snooze on a summer's day and a structure that will host a vine or flowering climbers.

TIME

A weekend (twelve hours for the woodwork and four hours for putting the pergola together).

USEFUL TIP

You will need assistance when putting the structure together – ideally two helpers.

YOU WILL NEED

Materials *for a pergola 2.55 m high and 3.59 m square. (All rough-sawn pine pieces include excess length for wastage.)*

- Pine: 4 pieces, each 3 m long and 75 mm square (main posts, and the 12 short linking posts that laminate and link the boat beams and top boards)
- Pine: 14 pieces, each 4 m long, 150 mm wide and 20 mm thick (top boards, boat beams, support boards)
- Pine: 4 pieces, each 2 m long, 50 mm wide and 30 mm thick (brackets)
- Pine: 6 pieces, each 4 m long, 30 mm wide and 20 mm thick (various temporary battens)

- Zinc-plated, countersunk cross-headed screws: 100 x 48 mm no. 8, 10 x 65 mm no. 10
- Brown preservative

Tools

- Pencil, ruler, tape measure, compass, bevel gauge and square
- Two portable workbenches
- Crosscut saw
- Electric jigsaw
- Large clamps: 4 clamps
- Cordless electric drill and cross-point screwdriver bit
- Drill bits to match screws
- Spirit level
- Electric sander with a pack of medium-grade sandpaper
- Paintbrush: 40 mm

COOL CANOPY

This project is made up from four posts set square to each other, with the top of the posts linked by two laminated "boat" beams on paired support boards, and six top boards crossing the boat beams at right angles. The boat beams are made by sandwiching the 300 mm-long linking posts between boards in such a way that the posts protrude at the top of the beam by 150 mm, providing link-up points for the topmost boards.

The structure is held square and prevented from wracking by eight brackets. We have allowed a good amount of extra length for the bracket pieces so that you can mitre the ends at 45° without worrying about cutting them too short. The ends of all the top boards are decorated with a classic cyma curve (an S-shaped detail), which can be cut easily with the jigsaw. The crossover of the boards at the corner posts, plus the addition of the top boards, results in a generous, bold structure which is really eye-catching. We purchased the wood ready-treated, and used the preservative to touch up the cut edges.

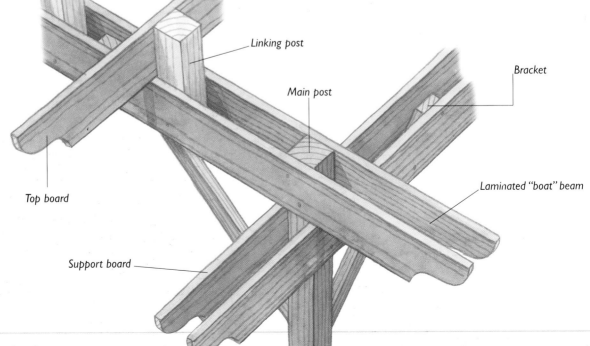

CORNER DETAIL OF THE CLASSIC PERGOLA

Linking post

Bracket

Main post

Laminated "boat" beam

Top board

Support board

Classic pergola

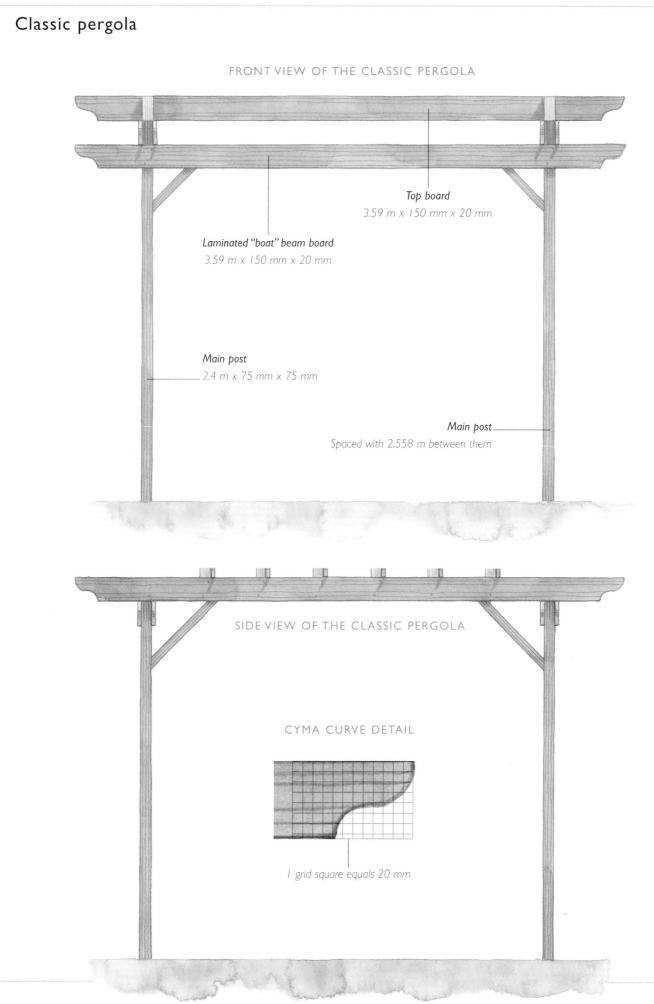

FRONT VIEW OF THE CLASSIC PERGOLA

Top board
3.59 m x 150 mm x 20 mm

Laminated "boat" beam board
3.59 m x 150 mm x 20 mm

Main post
2.4 m x 75 mm x 75 mm

Main post
Spaced with 2.558 m between them

SIDE VIEW OF THE CLASSIC PERGOLA

CYMA CURVE DETAIL

1 grid square equals 20 mm

EXPLODED VIEW OF THE CLASSIC PERGOLA

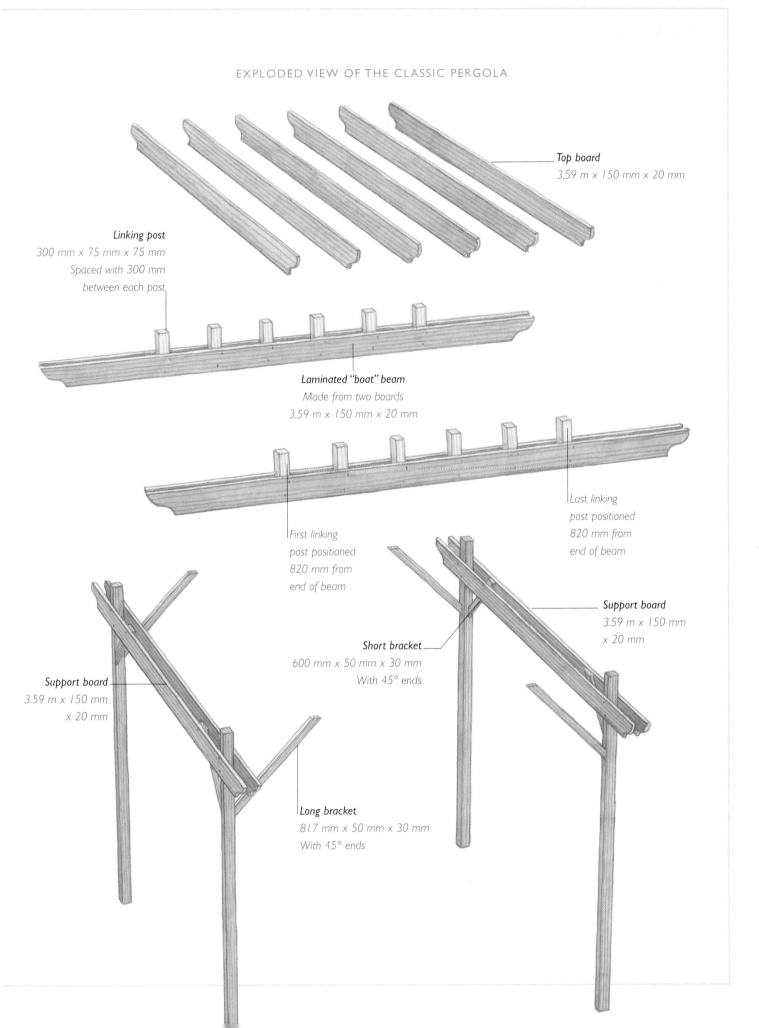

Top board
3.59 m x 150 mm x 20 mm

Linking post
300 mm x 75 mm x 75 mm
Spaced with 300 mm
between each post

Laminated "boat" beam
Made from two boards
3.59 m x 150 mm x 20 mm

*Last linking
post positioned
820 mm from
end of beam*

*First linking
post positioned
820 mm from
end of beam*

Support board
*3.59 m x 150 mm
x 20 mm*

Short bracket
600 mm x 50 mm x 30 mm
With 45° ends

Support board
*3.59 m x 150 mm
x 20 mm*

Long bracket
817 mm x 50 mm x 30 mm
With 45° ends

Step-by-step: Making the classic pergola

Jigsaw
Fit the jigsaw with
a new blade

Fixing
Run screws through
from both boards

Template
Use the
waste bit as a
template for
drawing the
other shapes

Workboard
Use a spare
piece of
150 mm-wide
wood as a
workboard

Clamp
Secure the post
with a clamp
and then screw
it into position

1 Use the crosscut saw to cut all the wood to size. Draw the cyma curve on the end of one of the fourteen top, boat and support boards, and fret out with the jigsaw. Use the waste as a pattern for the shape of all the other board ends.

2 Sandwich six of the 300 mm-long linking posts between two shaped boards to make a boat beam. Establish the position of the linking posts and clamp them in place. Run 48 mm screws through the boards and into the posts. Re-run the procedure to build the other boat beam.

3 Set the boat beam on the ground and screw the two main posts in place, using one 48 mm screw for each post. Link the bottom of the posts with a batten. Set a batten across the diagonal, make adjustments until the two diagonal measurements are identical, and screw it in position with 48 mm screws.

Temporary battens
The battens hold the arrangement square during construction

Helpful hint

Don't remove the temporary supporting battens until the main posts are securely in the ground, and the beams are braced with the brackets.

Assistance
You may need one or two people
to help you at this stage

4 Set the two-post boat-
beam structure upright and
use battens to prop it in place.
Check the vertical with a spirit
level. Make adjustments by
altering the position of the struts.

Spirit level
Check the
frame to
ensure that it
is upright
and square

Batten
supports
Use battens to
create tripod-
like supports

Clamp
Clamp the boards in place if you
have trouble holding them

Support boards
The paired
boards provide
extra support

Top boards
Butt each
board hard up
against the
linking post

5 When you have mounted both boat-
beam structures square with each
other, so they are well placed and upright,
link them with the two pairs of support
boards that run underneath the boat
beams. Screw the four support boards to
the main posts with 48 mm screws.

6 Fix the six top boards with 48 mm
screws. Cut the brackets to shape
(45° ends) and fix between the posts and
cross beams. Use 65 mm screws where
the brackets join the posts and 48 mm
screws where they join the beams. Sand
the pergola and paint it with preservative.

Inspirations: Pergolas

The visual impact of a structure clothed in flowers can be absolutely stunning. Perennials such as wisteria, roses, honeysuckle, clematis, passion flower, jasmine and climbing hydrangeas can be relied on to delight you every year. Annuals such as morning glory, sweet peas and nasturtiums can be grown to provide extra colour, or used to create a pergola that changes its coat each season.

ABOVE A pergola can be a frame for climbing plants, a focal point in a rose garden or a place for a swing. This rustic green wood pergola, with its decorative balustrades, makes an attractive addition to any garden.

RIGHT As well as supporting flowers, a pergola is perfect for grapevines or for creating a tapestry of exciting leaf effects, weaving the blazing reds of Virginia creeper, or various colours and shapes of ivy.

FAR RIGHT A pergola with brick pillars creates a traditional walkway, hosting plants such as wisteria, which has blooms that droop attractively through the beams. Scented roses make for an equally pleasant experience.

Victorian tool shed

This beautiful shed draws inspiration from a Victorian earth closet that I loved when I was a child. The proportions of the design make a garden shed that is just right for storing your lawnmower and tools. If you would like to build an attractive and practical tool shed that will impress your neighbours, have a go at this one.

YOU WILL NEED

Materials *for a tool shed 2.546 m high, 1.259 m wide and 1.230 m deep. (All rough-sawn pine pieces include excess length for wastage.)*

- Pine: 35 pieces, each 3 m long, 35 mm wide and 20 mm thick (frames for front, side, back, door and roof; braces for side and back panels; corner trim; doorway battens; roof support blocks; roof ridge boards; roof location bar)
- Pine: 6 pieces, each 3 m long, 150 mm wide and 20 mm thick (decorative barge boards, front feature boards, finial and floorboards)
- Pine: 2 pieces, each 2 m long, 50 mm wide and 30 mm thick (floor joists)
- Pine: 2 pieces, each 3 m long, 65 mm wide and 20 mm thick (ledge and brace details for the door)
- Pine feather-edged board: 60 pieces, each 3 m long, 100 mm wide and 13 mm thick (for cladding frames)
- Galvanized T-strap hinges: 3 hinges, about 250 mm long

- Galvanized sliding gate latch, complete with screws and coach bolts to fit
- Zinc-plated, countersunk cross-headed screws: 200 x 38 mm no. 8, 100 x 50 mm no. 8
- Galvanized nails: 2 kg x 40 mm x 2.65 mm
- Roof felt: 1.2 m x 300 mm
- Acrylic paint, colours to suit
- Clear preservative

Tools

- Pencil, ruler, tape measure, marking gauge and square
- Two portable workbenches
- Crosscut saw
- Cordless electric drill with a cross-point screwdriver bit
- Drill bits to match the screw, nail, dowel and vent hole sizes
- Small hammer
- Coping saw
- Electric jigsaw
- Small screwdriver
- Electric sander with a pack of medium-grade sandpaper
- Paintbrush: 40 mm

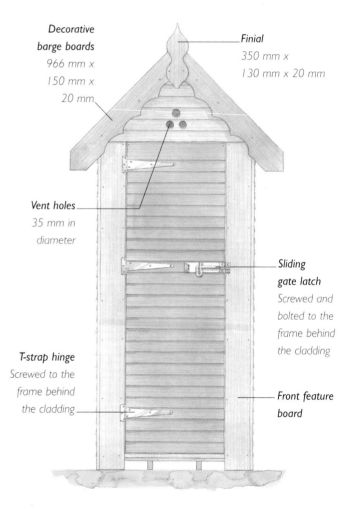

FRONT VIEW OF THE VICTORIAN TOOL SHED

Decorative barge boards 966 mm x 150 mm x 20 mm

Finial 350 mm x 130 mm x 20 mm

Vent holes 35 mm in diameter

Sliding gate latch Screwed and bolted to the frame behind the cladding

T-strap hinge Screwed to the frame behind the cladding

Front feature board

PRETTY AND PRACTICAL

The tool shed comprises four primary frames (the front, back and two sides), which are all made from 35 mm x 20 mm sections covered in feather-edged board. It has a steeply pitched roof sloping down at each side, a narrow door and airholes in the gable. The decorative details are made from 150 mm-wide boards. The floor is built directly on small-section joists, the idea being

you can mount the shed on blocks, a concrete base or slabs. The structure is designed so that two people can easily move the component parts to the site. The interior has been left plain, so that you can customize it to suit your own requirements. We are planning to fit an 150 mm-wide board for screwhooks and pegs to store the spade, fork, rake and so on. There will be an extra-strong hook for the mower, and a shelf at gable level for small items.

Victorian tool shed

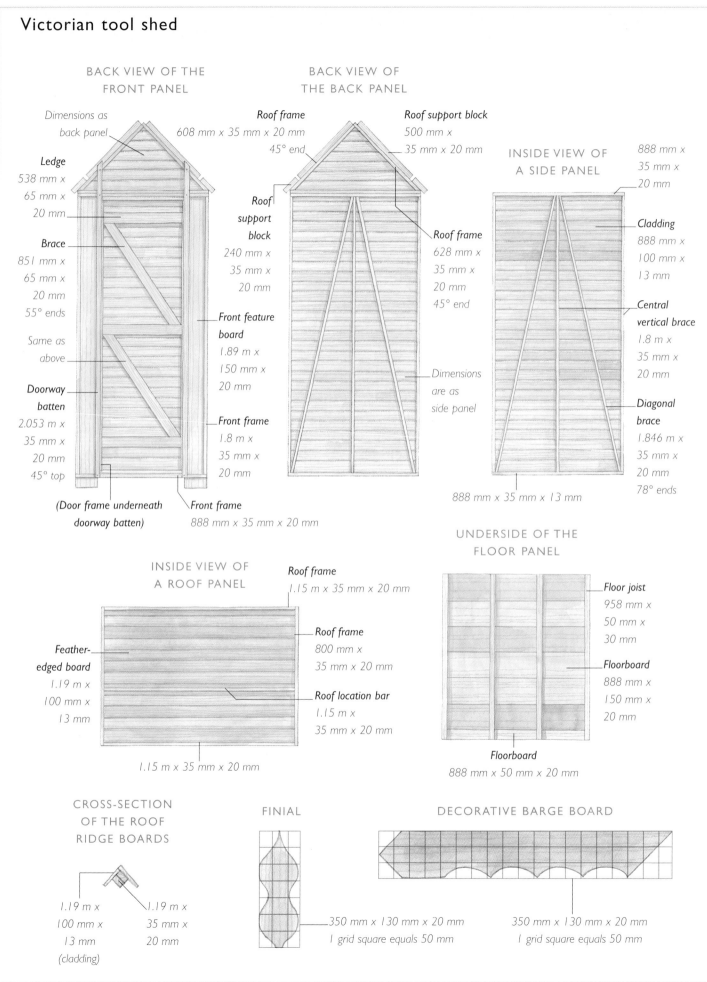

BACK VIEW OF THE FRONT PANEL

Dimensions as back panel

Ledge
538 mm x
65 mm x
20 mm

Brace
851 mm x
65 mm x
20 mm
55° ends

Same as above

Doorway batten
2.053 m x
35 mm x
20 mm
45° top

(Door frame underneath doorway batten)

Front feature board
1.89 m x
150 mm x
20 mm

Front frame
1.8 m x
35 mm x
20 mm

Front frame
888 mm x 35 mm x 20 mm

BACK VIEW OF THE BACK PANEL

Roof frame
608 mm x 35 mm x 20 mm
45° end

Roof support block
500 mm x
35 mm x 20 mm

Roof support block
240 mm x
35 mm x
20 mm

Roof frame
628 mm x
35 mm x
20 mm
45° end

Dimensions are as side panel

INSIDE VIEW OF A SIDE PANEL

888 mm x
35 mm x
20 mm

Cladding
888 mm x
100 mm x
13 mm

Central vertical brace
1.8 m x
35 mm x
20 mm

Diagonal brace
1.846 m x
35 mm x
20 mm
78° ends

888 mm x 35 mm x 13 mm

INSIDE VIEW OF A ROOF PANEL

Roof frame
1.15 m x 35 mm x 20 mm

Roof frame
800 mm x
35 mm x 20 mm

Roof location bar
1.15 m x
35 mm x 20 mm

Feather-edged board
1.19 m x
100 mm x
13 mm

1.15 m x 35 mm x 20 mm

UNDERSIDE OF THE FLOOR PANEL

Floor joist
958 mm x
50 mm x
30 mm

Floorboard
888 mm x
150 mm x
20 mm

Floorboard
888 mm x 50 mm x 20 mm

CROSS-SECTION OF THE ROOF RIDGE BOARDS

1.19 m x
100 mm x
13 mm
(cladding)

1.19 m x
35 mm x
20 mm

FINIAL

350 mm x 130 mm x 20 mm
1 grid square equals 50 mm

DECORATIVE BARGE BOARD

350 mm x 130 mm x 20 mm
1 grid square equals 50 mm

EXPLODED VIEW OF THE VICTORIAN TOOL SHED

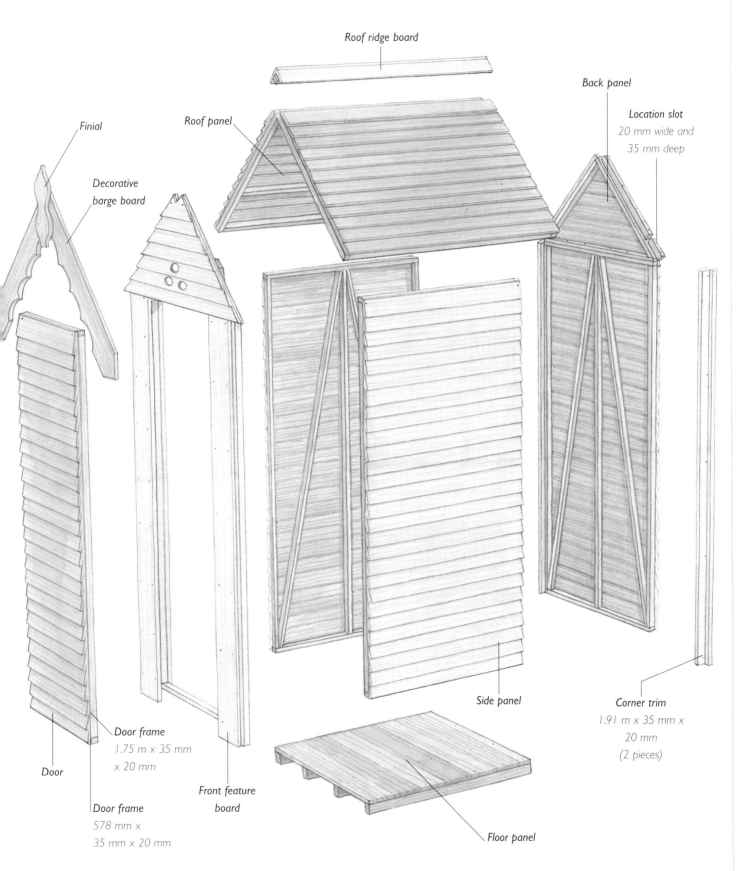

Roof ridge board

Back panel

Location slot
20 mm wide and
35 mm deep

Roof panel

Finial

Decorative
barge board

Door frame
1.75 m x 35 mm
x 20 mm

Door

Door frame
578 mm x
35 mm x 20 mm

Front feature
board

Side panel

Corner trim
1.91 m x 35 mm x
20 mm
(2 pieces)

Floor panel

Step-by-step: **Making the Victorian tool shed**

Knot-free wood
Make sure that the door frames are free from knots

Screwholes
Drill holes to take the screws

Uprights
Set the front frame and door frame pieces (for supporting the front feature board) 150 mm apart at the outside edges

Squareness
Set the frame square by checking that the diagonal measurements are identical

Tight fit
The braces should be cut to fit perfectly within the squared frame

1 Cut the wood to size. Take the lengths of wood that make the front panel, and butt joint them with 38 mm screws. Set the two 150 mm-wide front feature boards in place on the front of the frame (at either side of the door) and fix with 38 mm screws. Adjust for squareness. Screw the doorway battens on the back of the frame with 38 mm screws.

2 Build the back frame in much the same way as already described, only this time, fit a central vertical flanked by two diagonal braces. Aim to make the braces fit tightly into the frame. Build two identical side panel frames complete with central, vertical and diagonal braces, as described for the back frame.

Roof location bar
Set 500 mm from the ridge side of the frame

Screws
Have two screws at each joint

Check angles
Make sure the frame is a right-angled triangle

Roof frame
Choose an extra good bit of wood for the eaves

Roof support block
Fix each block with two 38 mm screws

Location slot
Use an offcut of wood to ensure that the location slot will take the roof panel

3 Build the door frame with the two sections of wood, using 38 mm screws, and 50 mm screws for fixing the diagonal brace pieces. Make two identical roof frames, each including a roof location bar, using two 38 mm screws at each joint.

4 Make two identical triangular gable frames with roof support blocks positioned to make location points for the roof frames. An offcut is used to ensure that the location slot is the correct size.

Cladding
The cladding needs to be level
with the top of the plate

Jig
Use a simple jig to help you
space the cladding properly

Coping saw
Cut the
cladding clear
of the roof
location slot

Nail holes
Drill holes
before nailing,
to avoid
splitting the
wood

Parallel
Check with a
tape measure
occasionally to
make sure that
the boards are
still parallel

5 When you have covered the gable frames by nailing on the feather-edged boards (a technique for positioning the boards is described in the Rabbit Ark project on page 98), use the coping saw to cut through the cladding to make a roof location slot, 20 mm wide and 35 mm deep, on the two elevated sides of the gable triangle.

6 Clad the other frames with feather-edged board. Use a simple jig to ensure that the overlap of the boards is constant. Drill holes for the nails, making sure that the nail doesn't pass through an underlying feather-edged strip. Use the jigsaw to make the decorative barge boards. Sand all the panels and paint them on the outside.

Fixing panels
Run screws
down through
the side panel
and floorboards
and into the
floor joists

7 Set the wall panels on the base and fix with 50 mm screws running into the floor joists. Locate the roof panels and screw in place with 50 mm screws. Wrap felt over the join between the two roof panels and fix with nails. Use 38 mm screws to fix the ridge board on top of the felt. Screw the decorative barge boards to the front edges of the panels, and the finials to the barge boards, with 38 mm screws. Drill three vent holes in the front gable. Fit the hinge and latch. Give all surfaces a coat of preservative. The floor panel should have an extra coat of preservative on the underside and on the ends of the joists.

Treehouse

Children love climbing trees, and will be absolutely delighted with this hideaway. In their imagination it may become anything from a hilltop castle to a pirate ship on the high seas, or a magic carpet gliding over cities and deserts. It also makes a perfect retreat for adults to escape the world! Select a sturdy, established tree.

FRONT VIEW OF THE TREEHOUSE

Panels
The roof and wall panels are constructed from 64 x 32 mm sections and then covered with feather-edged board

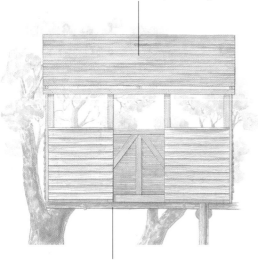

Support structure
This is constructed to suit the shape of the tree

A BIRD'S-EYE VIEW

The treehouse is made up from seven primary frames – two for the front, one for the back, one for each side, one for the base, and one for the roof. They are all made from 64 mm x 32 mm sections covered in feather-edged board. The roof slopes down towards the front, so that the overhang protects the inside of the house from wind and rain. The base is supported directly on beams that are fixed to the tree with coach screws if required. We were able to create a stable support structure with just three horizontal beams and two vertical poles, but you will need to build a support arrangement to suit the shape of your chosen tree. The whole structure is designed so that the frames can be built on the ground and then moved up into the tree.

The actual business of getting the structure into the tree is not only tricky, but also potentially very dangerous. You will need at least four strong people to help, plus a pair of ladders and lots of thick rope. You must all wear gloves and stout boots, and you should elect one person to lead operations. In the interests of safety, children and pets must be kept at a distance.

YOU WILL NEED

Materials *for a treehouse 2.267 m wide, 1.918 m deep and 1.910 m high. (All rough-sawn pine pieces include excess length for wastage.)*
- Pine: 25 pieces, 3 m long, 64 mm wide and 32 mm thick (long members for the frames for the walls, roof and floor)
- Pine: 20 pieces, 3 m long, 76 mm wide and 16 mm thick (floorboards)
- Pine feather-edged board: 30 pieces, 3 m long, 100 mm wide and 13 mm thick (wall cladding)
- Pine feather-edged board: 17 pieces, 3 m long, 200 mm wide and 13 mm thick (roof cladding)
- Pine: 2 pieces, 764 mm long, 100 mm wide and 13 mm thick (sills)
- Rope: 20 m, 10 mm in diameter (for lashing the floor panel to the support frame)
- Galvanized square-headed coach screws: 150 mm long, quantity as necessary (optional)
- Zinc-plated, countersunk cross-headed screws: 200 x 50 mm no 8, 200 x 65 mm no. 8
- Galvanized nails: 1 kg pack of 50 mm x 2.65 mm

Tools
- Pencil, ruler, tape measure, marking gauge, square and spirit level
- Two portable workbenches
- Ladder (length to suit site)
- Bolt wrench (if using coach screws)
- Crosscut saw
- Hammer
- Electric drill
- Cordless electric drill with a cross-point screwdriver bit
- Countersink drill bit to match the screw sizes
- Drill bit to match the size of the nails
- Drill bit to match the diameter of the rope
- Electric sander with a pack of medium-grade sandpaper
- Pair of clamps

Treehouse

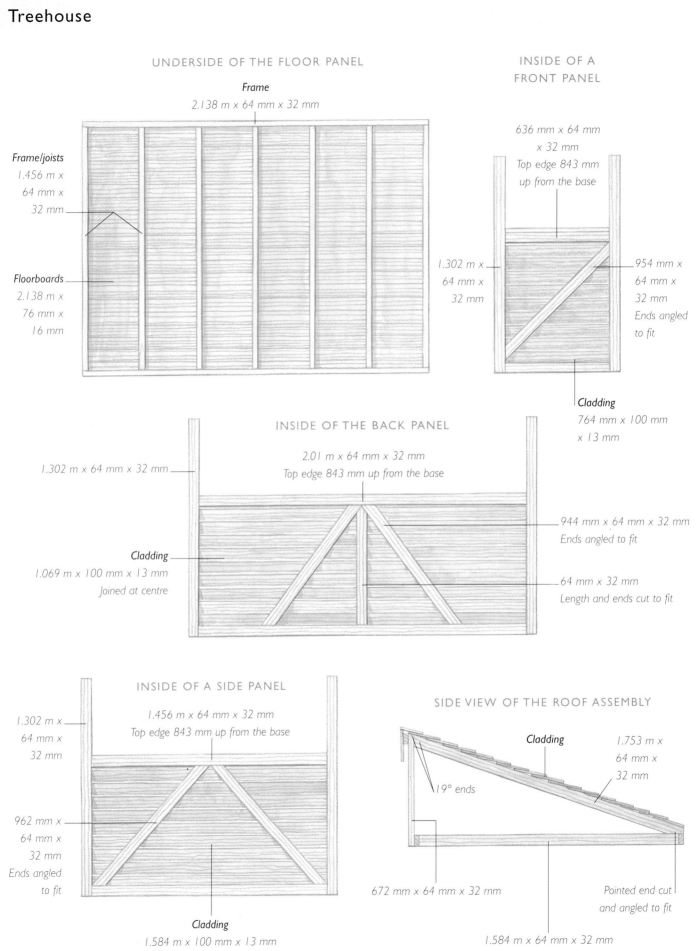

UNDERSIDE OF THE FLOOR PANEL

Frame
2.138 m x 64 mm x 32 mm

Frame/joists
1.456 m x
64 mm x
32 mm

Floorboards
2.138 m x
76 mm x
16 mm

INSIDE OF A
FRONT PANEL

636 mm x 64 mm
x 32 mm
Top edge 843 mm
up from the base

1.302 m x
64 mm x
32 mm

954 mm x
64 mm x
32 mm
Ends angled
to fit

Cladding
764 mm x 100 mm
x 13 mm

INSIDE OF THE BACK PANEL

1.302 m x 64 mm x 32 mm

2.01 m x 64 mm x 32 mm
Top edge 843 mm up from the base

944 mm x 64 mm x 32 mm
Ends angled to fit

64 mm x 32 mm
Length and ends cut to fit

Cladding
1.069 m x 100 mm x 13 mm
Joined at centre

INSIDE OF A SIDE PANEL

1.302 m x
64 mm x
32 mm

1.456 m x 64 mm x 32 mm
Top edge 843 mm up from the base

962 mm x
64 mm x
32 mm
Ends angled
to fit

Cladding
1.584 m x 100 mm x 13 mm

SIDE VIEW OF THE ROOF ASSEMBLY

Cladding

1.753 m x
64 mm x
32 mm

19° ends

672 mm x 64 mm x 32 mm

Pointed end cut
and angled to fit

1.584 m x 64 mm x 32 mm

EXPLODED VIEW OF THE TREEHOUSE

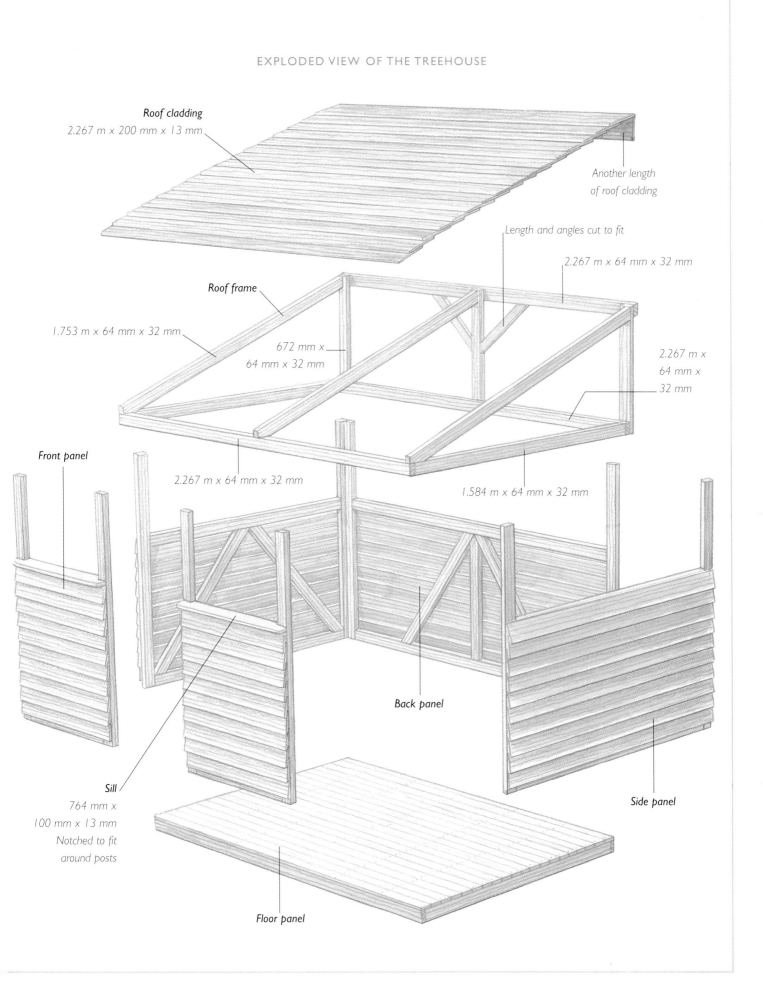

Roof cladding
2.267 m x 200 mm x 13 mm

Another length
of roof cladding

Length and angles cut to fit

2.267 m x 64 mm x 32 mm

Roof frame

1.753 m x 64 mm x 32 mm

672 mm x
64 mm x 32 mm

2.267 m x
64 mm x
32 mm

Front panel

2.267 m x 64 mm x 32 mm

1.584 m x 64 mm x 32 mm

Back panel

Side panel

Sill
764 mm x
100 mm x 13 mm
Notched to fit
around posts

Floor panel

Step-by-step: **Making the treehouse**

Support poles
Fix three or more poles to the tree
to make a horizontal platform

Rope-fixing points
Drill holes through the floor joists at
points for roping the floor to the tree

Branches
Trim off
branches that
will be in
the way

Square frame
Check the
frame is square
by comparing
the diagonal
measurements

Floorboards
All the boards
need to be
screwed to the
joists – one
50 mm screw
at each
intersection

1 Choose a strong, established tree with suitable branches. Prepare the site (the area within the tree) by cutting back branches if necessary. Build a sturdy support frame to make a platform for the treehouse. Wedge it between the branches or fix to the tree with coach screws if needed. Check that the supports are level.

2 To make the floor panel, first build a frame about 2.138 m long and 1.520 m wide, complete with secondary joists, using 65 mm screws. Screw on the 76 mm-wide floorboards with 50 mm screws. Drill rope-fixing holes through the joists at points where they will be useful for lashing the floor to the support frame.

Bracing
The diagonal struts reinforce
the frame and hold it square

Nailing
Nail the cladding to the
frame at every intersection

Cladding
Keep the
boards evenly
spaced and
parallel
(overlap the
boards by
at least
20 mm)

Corner joints
Fix the frame
together using
two screws at
each corner

Pilot holes
Drill holes for
nails (especially
those that
occur near the
end of a piece
of wood)

3 Using 65 mm screws, build the back wall frame, making it 2.138 m wide and 1.302 m in total height. Brace the bottom of the frame with two diagonals that centre on the underside of the top of the frame at sill level (no sill on back).

4 Fix the 100 mm-wide feather-edged board on the back wall frame. Working from the bottom upwards, and stopping short of the level of the sill, drill pilot holes through the boards and nail them to the frame with 50 mm nails.

Diagonals
Measure the diagonals to determine whether the frame is square

Brace
Fit a diagonal brace to hold the frame square

5 Build the frames for the other walls and roof in much the same way as already described, all the while double-checking that the measurements tally and the frames are square. Cut and fit two sills to the front frames with 65 mm screws.

Levelling
If necessary, add wedges under the base to make it level

Fixing
Thread rope through the holes in the joists and around the support beams

Additional support
We added vertical posts for extra strength

6 Heave the base up into the tree and lash it in place with rope. The rope allows the structure to flex in the wind without either the treehouse or the tree coming under too much stress.

Joining the panels
Screw the uprights to each other near the top, middle and bottom

Fixing to the base
Drive screws through the wall panel frames and into the base frame

7 Lift the two side wall frames up into the tree, clamp them to the base, and screw them in position with 65 mm screws. Remove the clamps. Repeat the procedure with the back wall frame.

Temporary stays
Remove stays after the roof is secured

Fixing the roof
Screw the roof frame to the top corners of the wall frames

Safety
Make sure that the ladder is positioned safely and ask a friend to help hold it in place

8 When the back and the two side frames are securely in place, hoist the roof frame into position and screw it to the corner uprights of the wall frames. Finally, screw the two front frames to the side walls and to the roof. Use 65 mm screws throughout.

Children's playhouse

This playhouse has wonderful decorative details, making it look as though it is straight out of *Grimm's Fairy Tales*, and is therefore guaranteed to stimulate children's imaginations. If you have children or grandchildren aged up to about twelve, they will find the playhouse great fun, and you will get much enjoyment from the project.

YOU WILL NEED

Materials *for a playhouse 1.91 m high, 1.844 m wide and 1.635 mm deep. (All rough-sawn pine pieces include excess length for wastage.)*

- Pine: 40 pieces, each 2 m long, 35 mm wide and 20 mm thick (frames, small trimmers, roof location bar, roof support blocks)
- Pine tongue-and-groove: 5 pieces, each 2 m long, 90 mm wide and 8 mm thick (stable door, decorative shutters, offcuts for glazing beading to fix the window)
- Pine: 12 pieces, each 2 m long, 150 mm wide and 22 mm thick (floorboards, decorative barge boards, decorative trim, back finial; offcuts for exterior glazing strip, window sill, door handle and door surround)
- Pine: 4 pieces, each 2 m long, 65 mm wide and 30 mm thick (floor joists, front finial)
- Pine: 4 pieces, each 2 m long, 65 mm wide and 35 mm thick (for covering the corners)
- Pine: 1 piece, 2 m long, 75 mm x 75 mm triangular section (roof ridge board)
- Pine feather-edged board: 100 pieces, each 2 m long, 100 mm wide and 10 mm thick (cladding; wall plates)

- Zinc-plated, countersunk cross-headed screws: 200 x 38 mm no. 8, 100 x 50 mm no. 8, 100 x 65 mm no. 10
- Galvanized nails: 4 kg x 40 mm x 2.65 mm
- Galvanized flat-headed 10 mm roof tacks: handful (to fix felt)
- Polycarbonate sheet: 330 mm x 345 mm (window)
- Piano hinges: 512 mm and 672 mm long, with screws to fit
- Water-based, exterior paint: matt white and blue
- Roof felt: 2 m long and 300 mm wide (for fixing under the roof ridge board)

Tools
- Pencil, ruler, tape measure, marking gauge and square
- Two portable workbenches
- Crosscut saw
- Cordless electric drill with a cross-point screwdriver bit
- Drill bits to match the screw and nail sizes
- Coping saw
- Electric compound mitre saw
- Hammer
- Electric sander with a pack of medium-grade sandpaper
- Paintbrush: 40 mm
- Pair of clamps

FRONT VIEW OF
THE PLAYHOUSE

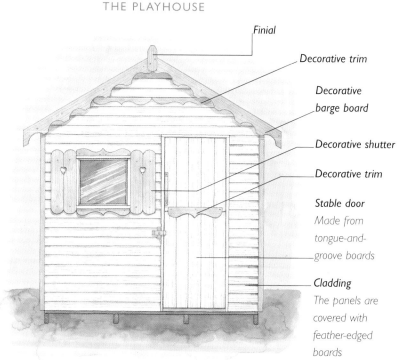

Finial

Decorative trim

Decorative barge board

Decorative shutter

Decorative trim

Stable door
Made from tongue-and-groove boards

Cladding
The panels are covered with feather-edged boards

A MINI HOUSE FOR MINORS

If you want to delight your children or grandchildren, you will happily spend a couple of weekends building this project. This is the playhouse that children dream about. It is high enough to stand upright in, the stable door can be shut from the inside, it has a proper weather-tight window, and there is plenty of space. The floor base measures 1.525 m x 1.255 m, so there is enough room for three or four children to spread out their sleeping bags. We have detailed the playhouse to suit children aged four to eight – with lots of fairy-tale trim and soft colours – but, for older children, the details can be changed and stronger colours used.

We have envisaged that you will make the frames outside your garage or garden workshop, and then move them to the site. We have fitted piano hinges because they close the gap between the door and the frame, preventing children from serious accidents to their fingers. Children can close the stable doors from the inside, but you can also open the playhouse from the outside.

Children's playhouse

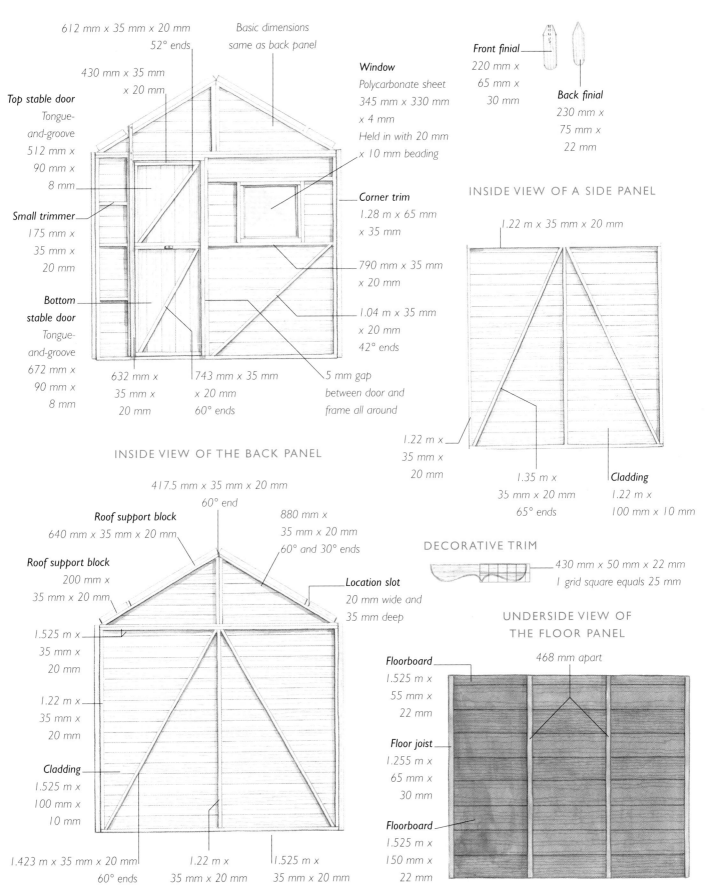

INSIDE VIEW OF THE FRONT PANEL

612 mm x 35 mm x 20 mm

52° ends

Basic dimensions same as back panel

430 mm x 35 mm x 20 mm

Top stable door
Tongue-and-groove
512 mm x 90 mm x 8 mm

Window
Polycarbonate sheet
345 mm x 330 mm x 4 mm
Held in with 20 mm x 10 mm beading

Corner trim
1.28 m x 65 mm x 35 mm

Small trimmer
175 mm x 35 mm x 20 mm

790 mm x 35 mm x 20 mm

1.04 m x 35 mm x 20 mm
42° ends

Bottom stable door
Tongue-and-groove
672 mm x 90 mm x 8 mm

632 mm x 35 mm x 20 mm

743 mm x 35 mm x 20 mm
60° ends

5 mm gap between door and frame all around

FINIALS

Front finial
220 mm x 65 mm x 30 mm

Back finial
230 mm x 75 mm x 22 mm

INSIDE VIEW OF A SIDE PANEL

1.22 m x 35 mm x 20 mm

1.22 m x 35 mm x 20 mm

1.35 m x 35 mm x 20 mm
65° ends

Cladding
1.22 m x 100 mm x 10 mm

INSIDE VIEW OF THE BACK PANEL

417.5 mm x 35 mm x 20 mm
60° end

Roof support block
640 mm x 35 mm x 20 mm

880 mm x 35 mm x 20 mm
60° and 30° ends

Roof support block
200 mm x 35 mm x 20 mm

Location slot
20 mm wide and 35 mm deep

1.525 m x 35 mm x 20 mm

1.22 m x 35 mm x 20 mm

Cladding
1.525 m x 100 mm x 10 mm

1.423 m x 35 mm x 20 mm
60° ends

1.22 m x 35 mm x 20 mm

1.525 m x 35 mm x 20 mm

DECORATIVE TRIM

430 mm x 50 mm x 22 mm
1 grid square equals 25 mm

UNDERSIDE VIEW OF THE FLOOR PANEL

468 mm apart

Floorboard
1.525 m x 55 mm x 22 mm

Floor joist
1.255 m x 65 mm x 30 mm

Floorboard
1.525 m x 150 mm x 22 mm

INSIDE VIEW OF A ROOF PANEL

DECORATIVE BARGE BOARD

Cladding
1.58 mm x
100 mm x
10 mm

1.02 m x
35 mm x
20 mm

Roof location
bar
1.54 m x
35 mm x
20 mm

1.54 m x 35 mm x 20 mm

1.121 m x 100 mm x 22 mm
60° ends
1 grid square equals 50 mm

EXPLODED VIEW OF THE CHILDREN'S PLAYHOUSE

Roof ridge board
2 m x 75 mm x 75 mm
triangular section

Back finial

Front finial

Wall plate
1.22 mm x
100 mm x 10 mm

Window shutter
Tongue-and-groove
450 mm x 90 mm
x 8 mm

Exterior
glazing strip
330 mm x
70 mm x
20 mm

Window sill
385 mm x
100 mm x
20 mm

Door handle
230 mm x 60 mm x 20 mm

Door surround pieces
1.2 m x 70 mm x 20 mm and
480 mm x 70 mm x 20 mm

Corner trim
1.28 m x 65 mm x 35 mm

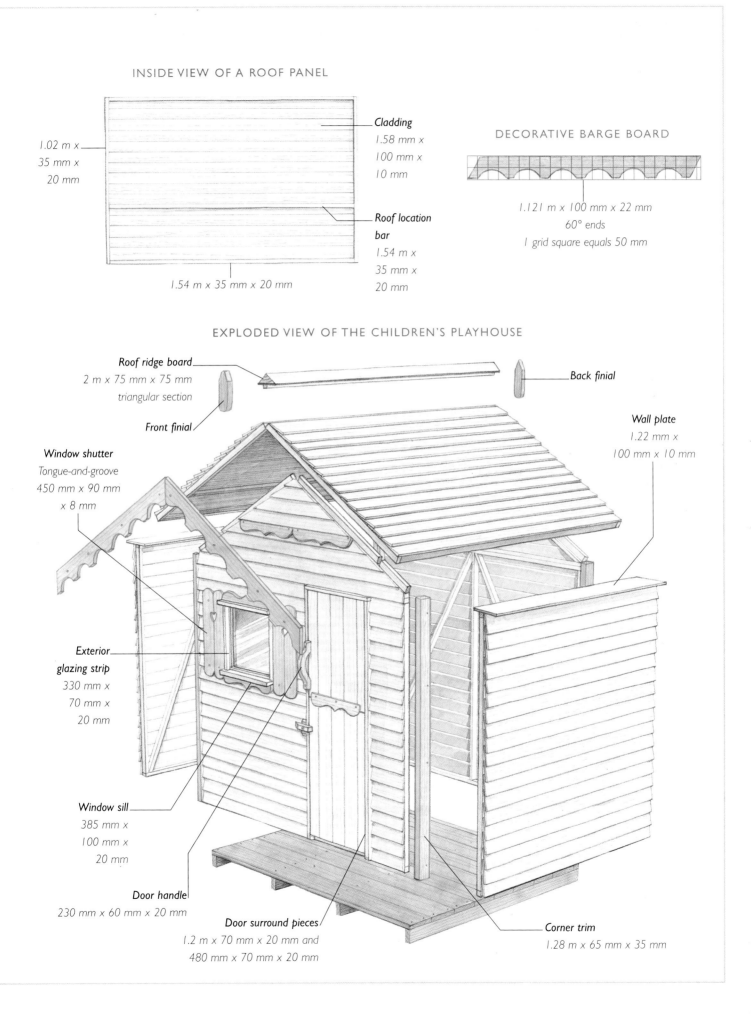

Step-by-step: Making the children's playhouse

Working area
Find an area of level
ground to work on

Wood selection
Make sure that the pieces that make
the door frame are perfectly straight

Screwholes
Drill holes at
the ends of
the boards to
take the screws

Joints
Use two screws
at the joints
where possible

Reinforcement
Use lengths of
spare wood to
strengthen the
hinge side of
the frame

1 Use the crosscut saw to cut all the wood to size. First, make the floor. Set the four floor joists about 468 mm apart and screw the 150 mm-wide floorboards in place with 50 mm screws so that you finish up with a base that measures 1.525 m across and 1.255 m from front to back.

2 Set out the overall size of the front frame and then divide it up, first with the two verticals for the door, then the two horizontals for the window, and so on. Finish with the diagonal braces and the small trimmers at the side of the door. Fix everything with 38 mm screws.

Verticals
Double up the
verticals for strength

*Roof support
blocks*
The blocks are
for locating the
roof panel and
need to be
placed
accurately

Overhang
The roof should mostly overhang at
the front and only a little at the back

Location slot
The roof panel
should drop
into position
and not need
to be forced

3 Build the gable triangles, complete with the roof support blocks (use 50 mm screws) for locating the roof frames. For the verticals, have two thicknesses of wood set back to back, in order to strengthen the frame and prevent it from twisting.

4 Screw the wall frames together with 38 mm screws and build the roof frame to fit. Locate the roof frame in the location slots that you have created on top of the gable frames. Dismantle the frames and lay them on the ground in readiness for cladding with feather-edged board.

Window frame
Cut the frame from
150 mm-wide offcuts

Turnbuckle
Make a turnbuckle from
a piece of spare wood

Appearance
Make sure
that the short
lengths of
cladding are
free from knots

Hinges
Put screws in
all the holes of
the hinges, as
they need to
be firmly fixed

Gap
Maintain a
5 mm gap
between the
two doors

5 First frame the window with exterior glazing strips cut from the 150 mm-wide offcuts, and then set to work covering the frame with feather-edged board, nailing it on with 40 mm nails. Clad the rest of the frames as described in other projects (a technique for positioning the boards is described in the Rabbit Ark project on page 98).

6 Build the frames for the doors (using 38 mm screws) complete with the diagonal braces, and cover them with the tongue-and-groove boarding. Fix the doors with the piano hinges and make the stops and turnbuckles from offcuts of 150 mm-wide wood (size and design to suit).

Heart detail
Push the two pieces together to
make the heart shape.

Painting
Sand and paint all the panels
inside and out before assembling

Screwholes
Drill holes for
38 mm screws
through the
cladding and
into the
frame behind

Placing
Make sure that
you align the
framework of
the panels
(rather than
the cladding)
with the base

Floor fixing
Screw down
through the
panel frame,
through the
floorboard
and into the
floor joist

7 Make the window shutters. Cut the heart detail (65 mm long and 50 mm wide) on the edges of the boards prior to assembly, using the coping saw. Cut the polycarbonate for the window "glass" to size and fix it with glazing beading strips taken from the tongue-and-groove.

8 Set the floor on site. Clamp and screw the walls in place with 65 mm screws. Position the roof frames, with the roof support blocks in the location slots. Screw on the wall plates with 38 mm screws. Nail the felt over the ridge and screw on the ridge board (50 mm screws).

Glossary

Aligning Setting one piece of wood against another (or one part of a structure against another) in order to obtain a good alignment or fit.

Butting The action of pushing one piece of wood hard up against another in order to obtain a good flush fit, with both faces touching.

Centring Setting a measurement or component part on the centre of another, or measuring a length or width to find the centre.

Cladding The procedure of clothing a frame with a covering of wood (such as a sheet of plywood, or a pattern of individual boards) as with the shed projects. Also the name for the wood used to cover the frame.

Colourwashing The technique of mixing paint with water and brushing the resultant wash on wood in order to achieve a delicate, stained finish.

Dry run Putting all the parts of a project together without glue, nails or screws, in order to see whether or not the components are going to fit. The procedure can also be used to check that the design is going to work.

Finishing The procedure of sanding, painting, staining and fitting hardware (wheels, latches, handles and hinges) in order to complete the project.

Hinging Fixing one part to another by means of a hinge, pivot, or rotating part.

Levelling Using a spirit level to decide whether or not a structure or component part is perfectly horizontal or vertical, and then going on to make adjustments to bring the component into line.

Marking out Using a pencil, rule, square and compass to draw lines on a piece of wood in readiness for cutting.

Preserving The procedure of painting wood with preservative in order to protect it against mould and rot. Preservative may be purchased as a colourless liquid, or it can form part of a paint or stain treatment. Some wood is pre-treated with preservative.

Sawing to size In the context of this book, the term mostly refers to the procedure of taking the sawn wood – meaning wood that has been purchased pre-cut to width and thickness – and cutting it to length.

Sighting To judge by eye. Also to look down a tool or down a length of wood in order to determine whether or not a particular cut, joint or structure is level or true.

Siting The act of walking around the garden and taking all the factors into consideration in order to decide whereabouts a structure is going to be placed.

Sourcing The process of making enquiries in order to ascertain the best source for wood, fixtures and fittings within your price range.

Squaring The technique of marking out with a set square or spirit level, and cutting and fixing wood so that surfaces or structures are at right angles to each other.

Tamping The act of using a length of wood to compact and level wet concrete.

Trial run Running through a procedure of setting out a structure – all the pieces of wood and the various fixtures and fittings – in order to ascertain whether or not the envisaged project or technique is feasible.

Trimming Using a cutting tool to bring a piece of wood to a good finish; also the act of using short lengths of wood to brace or strengthen a frame.

Suppliers

UK

Tool manufacturers

Black & Decker
210 Bath Road
Slough
Berks SL1 3YD
Tel: (01753) 567055

Stanley UK Ltd
The Stanley Works
Woodside
Sheffield
Yorks S3 9PD
Tel: (0114) 276 8888

Tool retailers

Tilgear
Bridge House
69 Station Rd
Cuffley
Herts EN6 4TG
Tel: (01707) 873434

S J Carter Tools Ltd
Gloucester House
10 Camberwell New Rd
London SE5 0TA
Tel: (020) 7587 1222

Sawmills & timberyards

Copford Farm Sawmill
Copford Farm
Dern Lane
Waldron
Heathfield
East Sussex TN21 0PN
Tel: (01435) 813472

Edward Hodgson & Son
    (Timber) Ltd
Silverdale Works
Silverdale Avenue
Liverpool
Merseyside L13 7EZ
Tel: (0151) 228 6328

Helmdon Sawmills Ltd
Weston Road
Helmdon
Brackley
Northamptonshire
NN13 5QB
Tel: (01295) 760305

Herriard Sawmills Ltd
The Sawmill
Herriard
Basingstoke
Hants RG25 2PH
Tel: (01256) 381585

General DIY Outlets
(branches nationwide)

B & Q plc
Head Office:
Portswood House
1 Hampshire Corporate Park
Chandlers Ford
Eastleigh
Hants SO53 3YX
Tel: (01703) 256256

Focus Do-It-All Group Ltd
Head Office:
Gawsworth House
Westmere Drive
Crewe
Cheshire CW1 6XB
Tel: (01384) 456456

Homebase Ltd
Beddington House
Railway Approach
Wallington
Surrey SM6 0HB
Tel: (020) 8784 7200

SOUTH AFRICA

Timber

DIY Superstar
11 Hornbee Street
Bloemfontein, 9301
Tel: (051) 430 4694

Cape Town Timber
86 Fitz Maurice Avenue
2 Eppingindustria
Epping, 7460
Cape Town
Tel: (021) 534 7201

Coleman Timbers (Pty) Ltd
Unit 3, 7 Willowfield Crescent
Springfield Park, 4091
Durban
Tel: (031) 579 1565

H & S Timbers
14 Wilstead Street
Benoni, 1501
Johannesburg
Tel: (011) 422 3223

Uitenhage Sawmills
148 Durban Road
Uitenhage, 6229
Port Elizabeth
Tel: (041) 922 9920

Tools and Hardware

Wardkiss Paint &
    Hardware Centre
329 Sydney Road
Durban, 4001
Tel: (031) 205 1551
(Outlets nationwide)

J & J Sales
38 Argyle Street
East London, 5201
Tel: (043) 743 3380

AUSTRALIA

DIY stores

Mitre 10
319 George Street
Sydney NSW 2000
Tel: (02) 9262 1435
(Outlets nationwide)

BBC Hardware &
    Hardwarehouse
Head Office, Bldg A
Cnr. Cambridge &
    Chester Streets
Epping NSW 2121
Tel: (02) 9876 0888
(Outlets nationwide)

Timber

ABC Timbers and
    Building Supplies Pty Ltd
46 Auburn Road
Regents Park NSW 2143
Tel: (02) 9645 2511

Finlayson's
135 Wellington Road
East Brisbane QLD 4169
Tel: (07) 3393 0588

Bowens Timber and
    Building Supplies
Support Office
48 Hallam South Road
Hallam VIC 3803
Tel: (03) 9796 3003

NEW ZEALAND

DIY stores

Mitre 10
Head Office:
182 Wairau Rd
Glenfield, Auckland
Tel: (09) 443 9900
(Outlets nationwide)

Placemakers Support Office
150 Marua Rd
Private Bag 14942, Panmure
Auckland
Tel: (09) 525 5100

Timber

South Pacific Timber
Cnr. Ruru and Shaddock Streets
Auckland City
Tel: (09) 379 5150

Lumber Specialties
117 Main South Road
Upper Riccarton
Christchurch
Tel: (03) 348 7002

Wilson Bros Timber
71 Foremans Road
Hornby
Tel: (03) 688 2336

Conversion chart

To convert the metric measurements given in this book to imperial measurements, simply multiply the figure given in the text by the relevant number shown in the table below. Bear in mind that conversions will not necessarily work out exactly, and you will need to round the figure up or down slightly. (Do not use a combination of metric and imperial measurements – for accuracy, keep to one system.)

To convert	Multiply by
millimetres to inches	0.0394
metres to feet	3.28
metres to yards	1.093
sq millimetres to sq inches	0.00155
sq metres to sq feet	10.76
sq metres to sq yards	1.195
cu metres to cu feet	35.31
cu metres to cu yards	1.308
grams to pounds	0.0022
kilograms to pounds	2.2046
litres to gallons	0.22

Index

Acknowledgments

AG&G Books would like to thank *Garden and Wildlife Matters Photographic Library* for contributing the pictures used on pages 50, 51, 74, 75, 106 and 107.